TOEFL
VOCABULARY
만점맞기 단어장

TOEFL VOCABULARY 만점맞기 단어장

지은이 서영국
펴낸이 임준현
펴낸곳 (주)넥서스에듀

출판신고 2008년 2월 18일 제311-2008-00008호 ①
121-840 서울시 마포구 서교동 394-2
Tel (02)330-5500 Fax (02)330-5557

ISBN   978-89-93164-01-5   13740

가격은 뒤표지에 있습니다.

저자와의 협의에 따라서 인지는 붙이지 않습니다.
잘못 만들어진 책은 바꾸어 드립니다.

본 책은 『TOFEL VOCABULARY 만점맞기』를
단어장으로 재구성했습니다.

www.nexusEDU.kr

TOEFL
VOCABULARY
만점맞기 **단어장** 〈〈〈〈〈〈〈〈〈〈〈〈〈〈〈〈〈〈〈〈〈〈〈

서영국 지음

넥서스에듀

TOEFL과 GRE를 수년간 학원에서 가르치고 있는 강사로서 적당한 토플 어휘집을 만들고자 토플 기출 단어들을 틈틈이 모으고 있던 중 마침 학생들의 바람이 있어 기존의 어휘집들이 갖고 있는 미흡한 부분들을 대폭 보강하여 어휘집을 내놓게 되었습니다. 기존의 어휘집들은 실제 시험과는 동떨어진 내용이 많았습니다. 이를 보완하기 위해 기획 단계에서부터 집필 마무리 단계까지 실제 시험을 치렀던 학생들과 여러 차례 회의를 통해 어휘 학습의 문제점과 효과적인 학습 방법에 대해 토론하고 학생들의 애로 사항 등을 참고해 기획에 반영했습니다. 이와 같이 학생들 덕분에 책의 방향을 잡을 수 있었다면 "장안의 명강사"로 불리는 동료 강사들은 오랜 현장 경험을 통해 전 제작 과정에 큰 도움을 주었습니다.

실제 시험에서는 한 단어가 가지고 있는 여러 가지 뜻을 묻는 문제가 나오지만 대부분의 책들은 동의어가 부족하여 문제 풀이에 어려움을 겪습니다. 풍부한 동의어의 제시는 비단, 동의어 문제뿐만 아니라 어휘 활용 능력을 키우는 데에도 중요합니다. 영어 단어에는 우리가 알고 있는 한 개의 뜻만 있는 것이 아니기 때문입니다. 문맥상에서 다양한 의미로 활용되기 때문에 영어 단어의 핵심적인 의미를 정확히 알고 여러 가지 유사한 의미로 확장하여 활용할 수 있는 능력을 키워야 합니다. 본 교재는 이와 같은 점을 보충하기 위해서 동의어를 풍부하게 제시했을 뿐 아니라 단어의 정확한 뜻을 이해할 수 있도록 유용한 어근 정리 및 영영풀이를 함께 실었습니다. 그리고 TOEFL이 미국 대학 교육을 이수할 수 있는 능력이 있는지를 측정하는 시험이기에 TOEFL에 분야별로 자주 출제되는 토픽과 관련어들을 정리해 놓았습니다.

시험을 치르는 수험생들의 입장을 충분히 고려해서 만든 본 교재를 통해 'TOEFL Vocabulary 만점맞기'를 성취하시기 바랍니다.

저자 **서영국**

1 **4주 완성**으로 구성된 **일일 학습**을 철저히 합니다.

4주 동안 1회를 학습하고 나면 형식상으로는 한 번이지만 내용상으로는
여러 번 반복 학습이 될 수 있도록 구성되어 있습니다.

2 제시되어 있는 다양한 **동의어**를 통해 그 단어의 여러 가지 뜻을 알아
둡니다.

여러 개의 동의어를 알아두면 다른 단어를 외울 때 이미 외운 동의어를 이
용해 일석이조의 효과를 볼 수 있습니다.

3 일일 학습 중간에 나오는 **어근 정리**를 잘 이용합니다.

어휘 실력도 늘리고 암기도 잘 할 수 있는 방법은 어근을 이용하는 것입니다.
어근을 이용하여 단어의 뜻을 유추할 수 있기 때문입니다.

차례

1st week

001 **prevail**
[privéil]

v. 우세하다, 널리 퍼지다
get control over; be greater in number, quantity, or importance

syn dominate, triumph 지배하다, 승리하다

In the end, these promising beliefs prevailed in their minds. 결국에는 이러한 긍정적 믿음이 그들의 마음을 가득 채웠다.

prevailing a. 널리 퍼진 syn. widespread, overwhelming, dominant, prevalent, rampant

002 **radical**
[rǽdikəl]

a. 근본적인, 급진적인
arising from or going to a root or source(basic); far from the norm

syn fundamental, essential 근본적인, 필수적인 **drastic, dramatic, extreme** (치료, 변화 등이) 격렬한, 극적인, 극심한

There was a radical difference between their views on the foreign policy. 그 외교 정책에 대한 그들의 견해에는 근본적인 차이가 있었다.

003 **accord**
[əkɔ́:rd]

v. 일치하다, 조화하다
conform or agree; grant, esp. as being due or appropriate; bring into harmony

syn agree, grant 동의하다, 승인하다

We should try to play the game according to the rules. 우리는 규칙에 따라 경기를 해야 한다.

according to ~에 따라서 syn. depending on
accordingly 그 결과로서 syn. consequently

Word Root	▸ cord = heart
concord	n. 일치, 화합
discord	n. 불일치, 불화

Similar Root	▸ sent = feel
assent	v. [제안에] 찬성하다
consent	n. 동의 [찬성]하다

dissent	v. 반대하다
resent	v. 분개하다
sentimental	a. 감정적인

004 express
[iksprés]

v. 표현하다
show a feeling, opinion, or fact by statement or art

syn **show, represent** 보이다, 표현하다 **communicate** 알게하다

I would like to express my thanks to my parents for their support. 나는 부모님께 나를 뒷받침해 주신 것에 대해 고마움을 표하고 싶다.

expressly ad. 명백히, 특별히 syn. explicitly

005 sustain
[səstéin]

v. 지탱하다, 유지하다, 지지하다
keep in existence; supply with necessities or nourishment; support the resolution of

syn **maintain, support** 유지하다, 지지하다

Only two of the planets could sustain life.
그 행성들 중 단지 두 행성에만 생물이 살 수 있다.

sustainable a. 지속(유지)할 수 있는, 환경 친화적인

006 even
[í:vən]

a. 변함없는, 공평한
having no variations; equal in degree, extent, or amount

syn **unchanging, plain, impartial** 변하지 않는, 평평한, 공평한

He was perfectly relaxed, and his breathing was quiet and even. 그는 완전히 긴장이 풀어져서 숨소리도 잔잔하고 골랐다.

007 susceptible
[səséptəbl]

a. ~할 여지가 있는, 쉽게 영향을 받는
capable of; easily influenced or affected

syn **prone, apt, likely** ~하는 경향이 있는 **possible (of)** 가능한, 허용하는 **easily affected by** 쉽게 영향을 받는

Police officers here are very susceptible to corruption.
이곳의 경찰은 부패에 노출되기가 매우 쉽다.

008 accommodate
[əkámədèit]

v. 적응하게 하다, 숙박시키다
make suitable; provide housing for

syn **suit, adjust, adapt** 조정하다, 적응시키다 **lodge** 숙소를 제공하다 **make room for** 수용하다

Designed by an Italian architect, the hotel can accommodate 600 guests.
그 호텔은 이탈리아 건축가가 설계했으며, 600명의 손님을 수용할 수 있다.

009 distinct
[distíŋkt]

a. 별개의
different in nature or quality

syn **characteristic, different, separate** 독특한, 구별되는, 분리된

The region linguistic and cultural identity is quite distinct from that of the rest of the country.
그 지역의 언어적, 문화적 성격은 그 나라의 나머지 지역과는 매우 다르다.

010 abundant
[əbʌ́ndənt]

a. 풍부한
present in great quantity

syn **large number of, numerous, plentiful** 많은, 풍족한

The lake attracts an abundance of wildlife.
그 호수에는 많은 야생 동물이 몰려든다.

abundance n. 풍요, 풍부함

011 covet
[kʌ́vit]

v. 몹시 갈망하다
wish for with eagerness

syn **desire, long for** 갈망하다 **envy** 부러워하다

She coveted his job so openly that conversations between them were tense.
그녀가 그가 맡은 일을 노골적으로 탐내는 통에 두 사람의 대화에는 긴장감이 돌았다.

Plus Data
covet a. 은밀한, 비밀스런 syn. secretive, implicit, private

012 emerge
[imə́:rdʒ]

v. 나타나다, 알려지다
rise from; become known

syn **appear, spring up** 나타나다 **become known** 알려지다

After a few weeks, the caterpillar emerges from its cocoon.
몇 주가 지나면 애벌레가 고치 속에서 나온다.

013 miniscule
[mínəskjùːl]

(or minuscule)

a. 아주 작은
very small

syn **tiny, minor, minute** 작은, 적은, 세세한

The film was shot in 17 days, a miniscule amount of time.
그 영화는 17일 만에 아주 짧은 기간 동안 촬영되었다.

014 draw
[drɔː]

v. 끌다
pull or direct something in a particular direction; attract attention

syn **attract, sketch, pull** 매혹하다, 스케치하다, 끌다

Our attention was drawn by the sound of gunfire.
총소리에 우리의 이목이 집중되었다.

Plus Data
drawback n. 불리, 결점 syn. disadvantage, weakness

015 ample
[ǽmpl]

a. 충분한, 큰
fully sufficient; of large or great size, amount, extent, or capacity

syn **sufficient, sizable** 충분한, 상당히 큰

There is ample evidence to prove his guilt.
그가 유죄라는 증거는 많다.

amplify v. ~을 확대[증대, 증강]하다

016 establish
[istǽbliʃ]

v. 설립하다, 확립하다
set up; make firm

syn **settle, confirm, constitute, organize, start**
설립하다, 확증하다, 구성하다, 조직하다, 시작하다

Mandela was eager to establish good relations with the business community. 만델라는 재계와 좋은 관계를 이루고 싶어했다.

017 flourish
[flə́ːriʃ]

v. 번창하다, 번성하다
grow or develop successfully

syn thrive, prosper 번창하다, 번성하다

Most plants flourish in this rich soil.
이곳의 비옥한 토양에서는 거의 모든 식물들이 잘 자란다.

018 obscure
[əbskjúər]

a. 애매한, 희미한
unclear and difficult to understand or see

v. 감추다
make unclear; conceal

syn ambiguous, equivocal, vague 애매한
uncertain 분명치 않은 dim 흐린 | conceal, darken,
dim, overshadow, eclipse, camouflage, cloak,
screen, shroud 감추다, 가리다

Details of this period of Shakespeare life remain obscure.
이 시기의 셰익스피어의 삶에 대해서는 자세히 알려져 있지 않다.

019 strike
[straik]

n. 파업
a group refusal to work

v. 때리다, 우연히 만나다, 생각나다
hit sharply or attack someone or something; come upon;
cause to think

syn work stoppage 파업 | hit, make contact with
때리다, 만나다

Sunlight filters through the clouds and strikes the surface,
which heats up as it absorbs the visible light.
태양이 구름을 뚫고 지표면을 내리쬐면 지표면은 가시광선을 흡수하면서 가열된다.

strikingly ad. 놀랍게도 syn. remarkably

Plus Data
boycott n. 불매 운동 sabotage n. 태업

020 substantial
[səbstǽnʃəl]

a. 많은, 중요한
large in size, value, or importance

syn large in amount or degree, abundant, ample,
considerable 많은, 상당한 actual 실제의 significant,
important, meaningful, notable 중요한

The study reveals very substantial differences between population groups.

그 연구에 의하면 인구 계층 사이에 상당한 차이가 드러난다.

021 substitute
[sʌ́bstətjùːt]

v. 대신 쓰다, 대체하다
put or use in place of another

syn replace, displace, take the place of, exchange 대체하다, 바꾸다

Instead of using silicon, they have substituted a more flexible material.

실리콘을 사용하는 대신, 그들은 좀더 탄력 있는 재료로 대체했다.

> Plus Data
> They substituted *nylon* for *silk*.(= 대신 쓰다)
> They substituted *silk* by(or with) *nylon*.(= 대체하다)
> 그들은 비단 대신 나일론을 사용했다.

022 speculate
[spékjulèit]

v. 깊이 생각하다, 추측하다
meditate on a subject; guess possible answers to a question

syn consider, meditate, contemplate 심사숙고하다 **hypothesize, guess** 추측하다

We can only speculate on the reasons for his sudden resignation. 그가 갑작스럽게 사임한 이유에 대해 우리는 추측만 할 따름이다.

023 stagger
[stǽgər]

v. 비틀거리다, 머뭇거리다
move or stand unsteadily; begin to lose confidence or strength of purpose

syn stumble, hesitate 비틀거리다, 머뭇거리다

She was coming back, staggering under the weight of a large suitcase.

그녀가 커다란 여행 가방의 무게에 치여 비틀비틀 걸어 오고 있었다.

staggering a. 비틀거리게 하는, 주저하게 하는, 깜짝 놀라게 하는
syn. hesitating, overwhelming, astonishing

024 scarce
[skɛərs]

a. 부족한
insufficient to meet a demand or requirement

syn rare, sparse 드문 **in short supply, insufficient**

결핍의 **infertile** 메마른

Fresh water and medicine were scarce in the flooded region. 홍수 피해 지역에 식수와 의약품이 부족했다.

Scarcely had the game started when it began to rain. 경기가 시작되자마자 비가 내리기 시작했다. (← 비가 오고 나서야 비로소 경기가 열렸다.)

scarcely ad. 거의 ~않다 syn. hardly, barely, rarely, seldom

---

025 slight
[slait]

a. 적은, 근소한
small in size, degree, or amount

syn **minor, minute, slender** 적은, 미세한, 가느다란

There was a slight increase in temperature last year.
작년에는 약간 기온이 올랐었다.

---

026 virtual
[vɚ́ːrtʃuəl]

a. [표면상은 그렇지 않으나] 실질상의
being in essence or effect though not in actual fact, form, or name

syn **(not perfectly but) almost actual, factual, practical, near, plausible, feasible** [말·진술 등이] 그럴듯한, 있음직한, 사실상, 실제의

The servants rarely leave the house and live like virtual prisoners. 하인들은 거의 그 집을 떠나지 않고 사실상 죄수나 다름없이 산다.

virtually ad. 거의, 사실상 syn. almost, in fact

> **Plus Data**
> virtual이 actual의 뜻이라면 virtual reality는 actual reality, 다시 말해 just plain reality이다. 하지만 virtual reality는 현실 세계가 아닌 '가상 세계'라는 뜻으로 통용된다. actual reality와 virtual reality가 다른 이유는 virtual이 almost actual이기 때문이다.

---

027 adapt
[ədǽpt]

v. 적응시키다
make suitable to

syn **adjust, accommodate, modify** 맞추다, 적응시키다, 수정하다

Courses can be adapted to suit the needs of each person.
학과목들은 개개인의 필요에 맞춰 조정될 수 있다.

adaptable a. 융통성 있는 syn. flexible

028 consequence
[kánsikwəns]

n. 결과
something that logically or naturally follows from an action or condition

syn **a result or effect of something** 결과
importance 중요성

She said exactly what she felt, without fear of the consequence.
그녀는 결과를 두려워하지 않고 느낀 그대로를 말했다.

consequently ad. 결국에 syn. later, finally

029 consume
[kənsú:m]

v. 섭취하다, 소모하다
take in as food; waste

syn **waste, spend, exhaust, use** 쓰다 **eat, ingest, swallow** 먹다

Many people have dramatically reduced the amount of red meat they consume.
많은 사람들이 붉은 고기(쇠고기, 돼지고기 등)의 섭취량을 크게 줄였다.

030 crucial
[krú:ʃəl]

a. 결정적인, 중대한
extremely important

syn **essential, important, substantial** 필수적인, 중요한, 상당한

We believe the question being investigated by the Commission is one of crucial importance to the country.
우리는 그 위원회가 조사하고 있는 문제를 우리 나라에 있어서 매우 중대한 사안이라고 생각한다.

Review

Monday

- ☐ prevail _____
- ☐ establish _____
- ☐ crucial _____
- ☐ adapt _____
- ☐ sustain _____
- ☐ even _____
- ☐ substantial _____
- ☐ accommodate _____
- ☐ distinct _____
- ☐ speculate _____
- ☐ scarce _____
- ☐ obscure _____
- ☐ consequence _____
- ☐ draw _____
- ☐ strike _____

- ☐ radical _____
- ☐ abundant _____
- ☐ emerge _____
- ☐ ample _____
- ☐ susceptible _____
- ☐ substitute _____
- ☐ flourish _____
- ☐ stagger _____
- ☐ covet _____
- ☐ slight _____
- ☐ virtual _____
- ☐ express _____
- ☐ miniscule _____
- ☐ consume _____
- ☐ accord _____

031-060

---

031 subsequent
[sʌ́bsikwənt]

a. 다음의, 그 후의
happening after something else

syn **later, afterward** 뒤의, 나중의

In subsequent interviews, Robert contradicted his original story. 나중에 한 인터뷰에서 로버트는 처음에 했던 자신의 말을 번복했다.

---

032 modification
[màdəfikéiʃən]

n. 변경, 수정
the making of a change in something

syn **alteration, change** 수정, 변경

The board has requested modifications of the rules.
이사회는 회칙 개정을 요청했다.

modify v. 수정하다, 바꾸다   syn. alter, change

---

033 attain
[ətéin]

v. [목적·희망 등을] 이루다
to succeed in getting something

syn **achieve, gain, reach, succeed** 성취하다, 얻다, 도달하다, 성공하다

Not all athletes attain this standard of physical fitness.
모든 운동 선수들이 이러한 신체 기준에 미치지는 못한다.

Word Root	▸ trin = get
abstain	v. 삼가하다, 억제하다 [abs=off, away]
contain	v. 포함하다 [con=together]
detain	v. 붙들다, 구류하다 [de=down]
entertain	v. 즐겁게 하다
maintain	v. 유지하다
obtain	v. 얻다, 획득하다
pertain	v. 속하다, 관계하다
retain	v. 보유하다
sustain	v. 떠받치다, 부양하다 [sus(=sub)=under]

034 float
[flout]

v. [물에] 뜨다, 떠다니다
not sink; move easily through

syn **stay on the top, drift, hover** 떠 있다, 표류하다, 머물다

Leaves and twigs floated on the water.
나뭇잎과 잔가지들이 물 위에 떠다녔다.

035 collaborate
[kəlǽbərèit]

v. 공동으로 일하다, 제휴하다
work together on a common enterprise or project

syn **join effort, work together** 공동으로 일하다

We have been collaborating closely with teachers in devising the lesson plans.
우리는 수업안을 짤 때 교사들과 긴밀하게 협력해 왔다.

collaboration n. 협력 syn. cooperation

036 detect
[ditékt]

v. 발견하다
notice something partly hidden or not clear

syn **discover, sense, recognize** 발견하다, 간파하다, 인지하다

I thought I detected a hint of irony in her words.
나는 그녀의 말에서 뭔가 모순된 점을 알아차렸다.

detectable a. 명백한 syn. apparent, obvious, noticeable

037 durability
[dʒùərəbíləti]

n. 내구성, 내구력
the ability to withstand hardship

syn **endurance** 내구성, 내구력

Finding a durable solution will not be easy.
장기적 해결책을 찾기란 쉽지 않을 것이다.

durable a. 지속적인 syn. lasting
duration n. 지속 기간 syn. length

038 exceed
[iksí:d]

v. 능가하다, 넘다
be greater than; go beyond a permitted limit

syn **surpass, go beyond** 능가하다, 넘어서다

Wind speeds exceeded 90 miles per hour.
풍속이 시속 90마일을 넘었다.

exceedingly ad. 대단히, 몹시 syn. extremely

Word Root	► ced, cess = go
access	n. 접근, 출입, 통로
accede	v. [요구, 제안 등에] 동의하다
cease	v. 그만두다, 중단하다
cede	v. [권리, 영토 등을 다른 나라에] 양도하다
concede	v. 인정[용인]하다
precede	v. [시간, 장소, 순서에서] 앞서다
proceed	v. 앞으로 나아가다
process	v. [식품을] 가공처리하다
recede	v. 물러나다, 퇴각하다
secede	v. 탈퇴[이탈]하다 [se=away, apart]
succeed	v. 성공하다, 계승하다

039 rudimentary
[rùːdəméntəri]

a. 기본적인, 초보의, 형성기의
basic; beginning; simple and not highly developed

syn **basic, elementary, simple** 기본적인, 초보의, 간단한

They were given only rudimentary training in the job.
그들은 업무에 필요한 기초 훈련만 받았다.

040 exception
[iksépʃən]

n. 제외, 예외
special case; leaving out

syn **exclusion** 제외, 배제

The children had shown exceptional courage.
그 아이들은 보기 드문 용기를 보여주었다.

exceptional a. 예외적인, 특별한 syn. unusual, extraordinary
exceptionally ad. 예외적으로, 특별히, 대단히 syn. abnormally, extremely

041 attribute
[ətríbjuːt]

v. [원인을] ~에 돌리다, ~의 탓으로 하다
think something is the result or work of something or someone

syn **ascribe** [원인을] ~에 돌리다, ~의 탓으로 돌리다

The job requires you to have personal attributes such as the ability to work as a team member.
그 일은 팀원으로서의 협동심 같은 개인적 자질을 필요로 합니다.

attributes n. 특질, 속성, 특성 syn. characteristics, personality, nature, trait, quality

Word Root	▶ tribute = give
contribute	v. 기여[기부]하다
distribute	v. 분배하다
tributary	a. 공물을 바치는, [강의] 지류의

042 tangible
[tǽndʒəbl]

a. 실체의
able to be experienced by senses; real or not imaginary

syn apparent, concrete 명백한 physical, material, touchable 유형의, 실체적인

The plan will bring tangible economic benefits to the area.
그 계획은 그 지역에 가시적인 경제 효과를 가져올 것이다.

043 apparent
[əpǽrənt]

a. 분명한, 명백한
easily seen or understood

syn clear, obvious, evident, definite 분명한 noticeable 눈에 띄는 perceptible 느낄 수 있는

The children's poor health was apparent from their physical appearance.
아이들의 부실한 건강 상태는 외모에서 뚜렷이 드러났다.

044 assume
[əsúːm]

v. [증거는 없으나] 사실로 생각하다
accept something to be true without question or proof

syn suppose, think, anticipate 가정하다, 생각하다, 기대하다

Scientists assume there is no life on Mars.
과학자들은 화성에는 생명체가 없다고 추정한다.

assumption n. 가정 syn. supposition

045 conspicuous
[kənspíkjuəs]

a. 뚜렷한, 두드러진, 뛰어난
easy to notice; very noticeable, attracting attention as by being unusual or remarkable

syn obvious, evident, noticeable 분명한 outstanding, eminent, prominent, distinguished 뛰어난 famous 유명한

She might have felt less conspicuous if there had been other women there too.
거기에 다른 여자들도 있었다면 아마 그녀는 주위의 시선을 덜 의식했을 텐데.

046 extend
[iksténd]

v. 뻗다, 넓히다, 확장하다
stretch or spread; enlarge; carry out further

syn **increase, stretch, outspread** 늘리다, 쭉 펴다, 넓히다

The company has recently extended its range of products.
그 회사는 최근에 생산 품목을 확대했다.

047 peculiar
[pikjú:ljər]

a. 별난
markedly different from the usual

syn **distinctive, extraordinary, strange, odd, unusual, eccentric, bizarre** 독특한, 특이한, 별난

He told me a most peculiar story.
그는 내게 아주 기괴한 이야기를 해주었다.

048 account for

v. 설명하다
tell the cause of

syn **describe, represent, explain** 묘사하다, 의미하다, 설명하다

You will be brought before the disciplinary panel to account for your actions.
너는 징계위원회에 회부되어 네가 한 행동에 대해 설명하게 될 거야.

049 considerable
[kənsídərəbl]

a. 상당한, 고려해야 할
large in number, amount, extent, or degree; worthy of consideration

syn **sizable, large, substantial** 상당한 **important, significant** 중요한

He has a considerable amount of money. 그는 돈이 상당히 많다.

> **Plus Data**
> considerate a. 사려 깊은 syn. thoughtful

050 property
[prápərti]

n. 특성, 소유물
a basic attribute in a substance; something owned

syn **characteristic, possession, estate** 특성, 소유, 재산

The books are my personal property. 그 책들은 내 개인 소유이다.

Tuesday

051 **obvious**
[ábviəs]

a. 명백한
easily perceived by the senses or grasped by the mind

syn **apparent, evident, manifest** 명백한

The influence of primitive sculptural motifs from the Pacific on the works of Epstein is obvious. 엡스타인의 작품에는 태평양 주변 지역의 원시 조각에서 발견되는 모티프의 영향이 분명히 드러난다.

052 **confine**
[kənfáin]

v. ~을 한정하다
place limits on

syn **limit, control, cramp** 제한하다, 통제하다, 속박하다

Many prisoners are confined to their cells for long periods of time. 많은 죄수들이 장기간 감방에 갇혀 있다.

confined a. 제한된 syn. limited, restricted

053 **dependable**
[dipéndəbl]

a. 의지할 수 있는
worthy of reliance or trust

syn **reliable, responsible, trustworthy** 의지할 만한, 책임감 있는, 신뢰할 만한

Many scientists have worked in the field with highly advanced and dependable machines for over seventeen years. 이 분야에서 많은 과학자들이 최첨단의, 신뢰할 만한 기계들을 가지고 17여년간 연구해 왔다.

Plus Data
undep_endable(↔ dependable) a. 믿을 수 없는, 부정직한, 허위의
syn. unreliable, untruthful, dishonest, lying, mendacious

054 **elaborate**
[ilǽbərət]

a. 정교한
finished with great care

syn **complicated, detailed, intricate** 복잡한, 상세한, 난해한 **sophisticated** 세련된

There are times when it is appropriate to have a more elaborate flower arrangement.
보다 더 공들인 꽃꽂이가 필요할 때가 있다.

055 rather
[rǽðər]

ad. 다소, 오히려
to a degree, on the contrary

[syn] **instead, somewhat** 다소, 오히려

The problem is rather more complicated than we have expected. 그 문제는 우리가 생각했던 것보다 좀더 복잡하다.

056 identical
[aidéntikəl]

a. 똑같은
exactly alike

[syn] **same, similar, duplicate, analogous** 유사한, 똑같은

All the plants were grown under identical conditions.
모든 식물이 동일한 조건 아래 재배되었다.

identify v. 확인하다, 구별하다 syn. distinguish, recognize, perceive, spot

057 pronounced
[prənáunst]

a. 두드러진, 입으로 말하여진
easily noticeable, strongly marked; spoken

[syn] **obvious, marked, significant** 분명한, 현저한

She still has a pronounced German accent.
그녀는 아직도 뚜렷한 독일어 억양을 갖고 있다.

pronounce v. ① 발음하다 syn. articulate, enunciate, vocalize
② 선언하다 syn. assert, declare

Word Root	▶ nounce, nounci = say
announce	v. 발표하다, 알리다
denounce	v. 공공연히 비난하다, 고발하다
renounce	v. [권리 등을] 포기하다, 부인하다
enunciate	v. 말하다, 발음하다

058 barren
[bǽrən]

a. 불모의, 임신 못 하는
incapable of sustaining life

[syn] **infertile, sterile, lifeless** 메마른, 불모의, 생물이 살지 않는

This land is a remote and barren place.
이 땅은 외지고 척박한 곳이다.

Plus Data
fertile(↔ barren) a. 비옥한, 다산(多産)의 syn. fruitful, productive, prolific

059 **eventually**
[ivéntʃuəli]

ad. 마침내, 결국에는
in the end after a long time or a lot of effort

syn **finally, later** 마침내, 결국에는

Dad was eventually diagnosed as suffering from a chronic heart condition.
아빠는 결국 만성 심장 질환을 앓고 있다는 진단을 받았다.

060 **fundamental**
[fʌ̀ndəméntl]

a. 기본적인, 근본적인
serving as an essential component

syn **basic, essential, principal** 기본적인, 근본적인, 필수적인, 주요한

Some people see this as a fundamental flaw in his argument. 어떤 사람들은 이것을 그의 주장에 있는 근본적인 오류라고 생각한다.

Review

 Tuesday

□ elaborate _____

□ account for _____

□ considerable _____

□ fundamental _____

□ collaborate _____

□ extend _____

□ durability _____

□ exceed _____

□ rudimentary _____

□ rather _____

□ peculiar _____

□ tangible _____

□ apparent _____

□ identical _____

□ eventually _____

□ detect _____

□ attribute _____

□ attain _____

□ exception _____

□ property _____

□ obvious _____

□ modification _____

□ dependable _____

□ subsequent _____

□ assume _____

□ confine _____

□ pronounced _____

□ barren _____

□ float _____

□ conspicuous _____

061-090

---

061 **tiny**
[táini]

a. 작은
very small

syn **little, extremely small, minuscule, minute**
아주 작은

She is one of a tiny minority of female journalists.
그녀는 극히 얼마 안 되는 여성 저널리스트 중의 한 명이다.

---

062 **massive**
[mǽsiv]

a. 육중한, 대규모의
very large in size, amount, or number

syn **colossal, enormous, huge, vast, substantial, considerable, gigantic** 거대한

He had a massive amount of money. But he lost it through gamble. 그는 상당한 돈을 갖고 있었지만 도박으로 날려버렸다.

---

063 **facilitate**
[fəsílətèit]

v. 용이하게 하다
be of use; make easy

syn **make more available, aid, make easy** 개량하다, 돕다, 쉽게 하다

The counselor may be able to facilitate communication between the couple.
상담원이 그 부부 간의 대화를 원활하게 해 줄 수 있을 것이다.

Word Root ▸ fac/fact, fec/fect, fic/fict = make
artifact   n. 인공물 [art=skill]
factor   n. 요소, 요인
factual   a. 사실에 입각한
faculty   n. 능력, 교수진
manufacture   v. 제작[생산]하다
affect   v. ~에 영향을 미치다
defect   v. 이탈하다
effect   v. 초래하다
infect   v. ~에 감염시키다
perfect   v. 완전히 하다; 완전한
beneficial   a. 유리한
fiction   n. 허구, 소설, 이야기

proficient	a. 능숙한, 숙달된
suffice	v. 충분하다, 만족시키다 [suf〈sub=under]
superficial	a. 표면의, 외면의 [super=above, over]
sacrifice	v. 희생하다

064 launch
[lɔːntʃ]

v. 진수하다, 시작하다
take off or begin

syn **launch, initiate, commence, take off** 시작하다
establish 설립하다 **project** 발사하다

The agency will launch a new weather satellite next
month. 그 기관은 다음 달에 새 기상 위성을 발사할 것이다.

065 abrupt
[əbrʌ́pt]

a. 갑작스러운
exceedingly sudden and unexpected

syn **sudden, sharp** 갑작스러운

Our friendship came to an abrupt end.
우리의 우정은 갑작스레 끊어졌다.

abruptly ad. 갑자기 syn. suddenly

Word Root	▶ rupt = break
bankrupt	a. 파산한, 지급능력이 없는 [bank=은행]
corrupt	v. 부패시키다 [cor〈con=together]
erupt	v. [화산 등이] 폭발하다
disrupt	v. 분열시키다, 막다
interrupt	v. 중단시키다, 가로막다 [inter=between]
rupture	n. 파열, 불화

066 bulk
[bʌlk]

n. 큰 크기, 부피
something or someone that is very large

syn **main part, majority** 대부분 **large size, great
quantity** 큰 크기, 부피

Women still undertake the bulk of domestic work in the
home. 아직도 여성들이 집에서 많은 가사 노동을 떠맡고 있다.

067 spawn
[spɔːn]

v. 생기게 하다, 낳다
call forth; cause something new to grow suddenly

syn **produce, create, engender, generate** 생산하다

multiply, proliferate, reproduce 증산하다, 확산하다

The book was a fantastic success, spawning a hit TV series. 그 책은 커다란 성공을 거두어 인기 텔레비전 시리즈를 탄생시켰다.

068 **intricate**
[íntrikət]

a. 복잡한, 뒤얽힌, 난해한
having many complexly interrelating parts

[syn] **complex, complicated** 복잡한 **sophisticated, elaborate** 정교한, 세련된

Nature has an intricate pattern of birds and flowers.
자연은 새와 꽃이라는 절묘한 어울림을 가지고 있다.

069 **link**
[liŋk]

v. 연결하다
cause to be or become joined or united

[syn] **connect** 잇다, 연결하다 **relate** 연관짓다

Police suspect that the two murder cases are linked.
경찰은 두 살인 사건이 관련되어 있다고 의심하고 있다.

linked a. 관련된 syn. put together, related

070 **extensive**
[iksténsiv]

a. 포괄적인, 광범위한, 넓은
great in range or scope

[syn] **wide, far-reaching, large, far-embracing, comprehensive, expansive** 광범위한, 포괄적인

She has an extensive knowledge of art history.
그녀는 예술사에 해박한 지식을 가지고 있다.

> **Plus Data**
> **extend** v. ① 늘이다 syn. elongate, enlarge, lengthen, prolong, stretch
> ② 증가하다 syn. augment, broaden, expand, increase
> **expensive** a. 값비싼, 사치스런 syn. costly, dear, excessive, exorbitant, extravagant

071 **tricky**
[tríki]

a. 까다로운, 교활한
difficult to deal with; deceptive

[syn] **difficult, challenging, complicated, intricate** 힘이 드는 **crafty, cunning, sly, wily, deceitful, deceptive** 교활한, 사기의

That is a tricky question because there are many things

to consider. 고려해야 할 것이 많기 때문에 그것은 까다로운 질문이다.

trick n. 사기 syn. deception, hoax

Word Root	▶ cept, ceiv, ceit = take
conceive	v. [생각, 계획 등을] 마음에 품다, 구상하다
deceive	v. 속이다
perceive	v. 지각[인식]하다
receive	v. 받다

---

072 **imposing**
[impóuziŋ]

a. 인상적인, 당당한
having an appearance which looks important or causes admiration

syn **impressive, striking, stately, dignified, grand, majestic** 인상적인, 위엄 있는

He was an imposing figure on stage.
그는 무대에서 중요한 인물이었다.

impose v. 부과하다, 덧붙이다 syn. force upon, levy, add, tax

Plus Data
an imposing air 당당한 태도

---

073 **sporadic**
[spərǽdik]

a. 산발적인, 산재하는, 돌발적인
recurring irregularly

syn **intermittent** 간헐성의, 때때로 중단되는 **infrequent, periodical, irregular** 불규칙적인

We've had only sporadic snow in this month.
요번 달에는 가끔씩만 눈이 왔다.

---

074 **coherent**
[kouhíərənt]

a. 밀착하는, 일관성 있는, 조리 있는
sticking together; logically ordered or integrated

syn **logical, reasoning, reasonable** 논리적인, 이성적인, 합리적인

The writer presents this complex character as a coherent whole. 작가는 이 복잡 다단한 인물을 일관성 있는 존재로 다루고 있다.

cohesion n. 결합, 응집력 syn. unity

075 comprehend
[kàmprihénd]

v. 이해하다
get the meaning of something

syn **understand** 이해하다 **grasp, perceive, absorb** 감지하다

How could you possibly comprehend the difficulties of my situation? 네가 어떻게 내가 처한 어려운 상황을 이해할 수 있겠니?

comprehensible a. 이해할 수 있는 syn. apprehensible, understandable

comprehensive a. 포괄적인 syn. extensive, wide, far-reaching, large, far-embracing

Word Root	▸ prehens, prehend = take
apprehend	v. 체포하다, 염려하다
comprehensive	a. 포괄적인, 포용력이 큰
reprehend	v. 꾸짖다, 비난하다

076 spectacular
[spektǽkjulər]

a. 장관의
sensational in appearance or thrilling in effect

syn **impressive, marvelous, magnificent, sensational, thrilling** 장관의, 놀랄 만한

The show was a spectacular success. 그 공연은 대성공이었다.

077 jeopardize
[dʒépərdàiz]

v. 위태롭게 하다
pose a threat to, put at risk

syn **threaten, endanger, peril, hazard, risk** 위협하다, 위태롭게 하다

Cuts in funding could jeopardize this vital research work. 예산 삭감이 이 중요한 연구를 망쳐버릴 수 있다.

078 adjacent
[ədʒéisnt]

a. 인접한, 부근의
near or close to

syn **nearby, neighboring, adjoining, bordering** 인접한, 불굴의

The site of the new building is adjacent to the park. 새 빌딩이 들어설 곳은 공원에 가깝다.

079 surge
[səːrdʒ]

v. 파도처럼 밀려오다
increase suddenly and greatly; rise and move in waves
n. 쇄도
a sudden and great increase

syn **increase suddenly** 갑자기 증대하다 **rise, rush**
밀어닥치다 | **flood, rush, torrent, wave, acceleration,**
emergence 쇄도

The crowd surged forward toward the police.
군중이 경찰을 향해 물밀 듯 몰려왔다.

surging a. 늘어난, 증가된 syn. accelerating

080 approach
[əpróutʃ]

v. ~에 다가가다
move toward

syn **move toward, advance, approximate** 다가가다,
이동하다 | **method, access, passageway, strategy**
접근법

We need a fresh approach to sports in education.
우리는 교육과정에서 가르치는 스포츠에 새로이 접근해야 한다.

081 accomplish
[əkʌ́mpliʃ]

v. 이루다, 완수하다
gain with effort

syn **achieve, perform, fulfill** 이루다 **execute** 수행하다

We didn't accomplish much at work this week.
이번 주에는 별로 일을 많이 하지 못했다.

accomplished a. 능란한, 뛰어난, 성취된 syn. skilled

Word Root	▶ pli, ply, ple, plet = fill
compliment	n. v. 칭찬[하다]
complement	n. v. 보완[하다]
complete	a. 완전한 v. 완성하다
deplete	v. 고갈시키다
implement	n. 도구 v. 약속을 이행하다
supplement	n. v. 보충[하다]
supply	v. 공급하다

082 consist of

v. ~로 구성되다
be composed of

syn **be made up of, be composed of, comprise**
~으로 구성되다

His breakfast consists of dry bread and a cup of tea.
그의 아침 식사는 마른 빵과 차 한 잔이다.

consistently ad. 시종일관하여 syn. regularly

083 **exploit**
[éksplɔit]

v. 이용하다
make good use of

syn **use, employ, utilize** 활용하다, 이용하다, 착취하다
manipulate 조정[조작]하다

Children are being exploited in many of these factories.
아이들이 이러한 여러 군데의 공장에서 착취당하고 있다.

084 **maintain**
[meintéin]

v. 유지하다
keep in a certain state

syn **preserve, keep, sustain** 보전하다, 유지하다

Some schools experienced difficulty in maintaining staffing
levels. 몇몇 학교들은 수준 있는 교직원을 확보하는 데 어려움을 겪었다.

085 **release**
[rilíːs]

v. 놓아주다, 공개하다
make free; allow something to be shown in public or to be
available for use

syn **give off, emit** 내뿜다 **discharge, free, liberate**
해방하다

The authorities had recently released two political
prisoners. 당국은 최근 두 명의 정치범을 석방했다.

086 **variety**
[vəràiəti]

n. 다양함, 차이, 종류
diversity; difference; specific kind of something

syn **diversity** 다양성 **kind, species, type** 종류

We want to hear the opinions of a variety of people.
우리는 다양한 사람들로부터 의견을 듣고자 한다.

various a. 다양한, 많은 syn. differing, diverse, miscellaneous,
countless, many, myriad, numerous, several
vary v. 변화를 주다, 바꾸다 syn. change, alter, modify, transform

087 **accompany**
[əkʌ́mpəni]

v. 동행하다, 수반하다
be associated with; go or travel with

syn occur with, travel with 동반하다, 따라가다

Children under 12 must be accompanied by an adult.
12세 이하의 어린이는 보호자를 대동해야 한다.

---

088 **adverse**
[ædvə́:rs]

a. 반대[적대]하는, 불리한
acting against or in an opposing direction; contrary to one interests

syn detrimental 유해한 negative, opposing, opposite, contrary, converse, reverse 반대하는 hostile 적대하는

Ironically, the newly elected president received an adverse reaction from the public.
아이러니하게도 새로 당선된 대통령은 대중으로부터 적대적인 반응을 얻었다.

adversely ad. 반대로, 적대적으로 syn. negatively

Word Root	▶ vert, vers = turn
avert	v. [눈, 얼굴, 생각 등을] 돌리다, [위험을] 피하다
adversary	n. 적, 상대자
converse	a. 거꾸로 n. 반대
convert	v. 개종[전환]하다
controvert	v. 반박[논쟁]하다
controversy	n. 논쟁, 논의
incontrovertible	a. 논쟁의 여지가 없는
invert	v. 뒤집다
revert	v. [원상태로] 되돌아가다
subvert	v. [종교, 정부를] 파괴하다, 전복시키다 [sub=below]
vertical	a. 수직의, 바로선

---

089 **allocate**
[ǽləkèit]

v. 배분하다, 배치하다
to distribute according to a plan

syn designate 지정하다 allot, assign 할당하다 distribute, dispense 분배하다

Our task is to decide the best way to allocate scarce resources. 우리의 업무는 부족한 자원을 분배하는 최적의 방법을 찾는 것이다.

---

090 **delicate**
[délikət]

a. 섬세한
needing careful treatment, easily damaged

syn sensitive, subtle, dainty, careful 민감한, 섬세한, 조심스러운

I admired your delicate handling of the situation.
그 상황을 조심스럽게 잘 처리하셨군요.

Review

☐ maintain

☐ jeopardize

☐ adjacent

☐ launch

☐ allocate

☐ adverse

☐ accomplish

☐ variety

☐ link

☐ spectacular

☐ tricky

☐ imposing

☐ sporadic

☐ accompany

☐ delicate

☐ massive

☐ tiny

☐ abrupt

☐ facilitate

☐ approach

☐ spawn

☐ surge

☐ exploit

☐ bulk

☐ coherent

☐ intricate

☐ comprehend

☐ extensive

☐ release

☐ consist of

091-120

091 generate
[dʒénərèit]

v. 낳다, 발생시키다
bring into existence

syn **produce, create, form, make** 만들다

The new car factory will generate a lot of jobs in the area.
신설된 자동차 공장은 이 지역에 많은 일자리를 창출해 낼 것이다.

Word Root	▶ gen = birth, creation, race, kind
congenial	a. 같은 성질의, 마음이 맞는
congenital	a. [병 따위가] 선천적인
degenerate	v. 타락[퇴보]하다
engender	v. 발생시키다, 야기하다
homogeneous	a. 동종의
ingenious	a. [사람이] 영리한
indigenous	a. 토착의, 고유한

092 celebrated
[séləbrèitid]

a. 유명한
widely known and esteemed

syn **famous, noted, renowned, acknowledged, outstanding, distinguished, conspicuous, eminent, prominent, noticeable, perceptible** 유명한, 뛰어난, 두드러진

Although he had many weaknesses, he became a celebrated artist. 그는 결점이 많았지만 유명한 예술가가 되었다.

celebrity n. 유명 인사 syn. famous person

093 subsidize
[sʌ́bsidàiz]

v. 보조금을 지급하다
to pay part of the cost of something

syn **finance, fund** 자금을 공급하다 **assist, back** 돕다

The government has said it would no longer subsidize public transportation.
정부는 더 이상 대중 교통을 위해 재정 지원을 하지 않겠다고 밝혔다.

094 rigorous
[rígərəs]

a. 엄격한, 엄밀한
demanding strict attention to rules

syn **severe, harsh, demanding** 엄격한, 가혹한, 큰 노력이 드는

The work failed to meet their rigorous standards.
그 작품은 그들의 엄격한 기준을 충족시키지 못했다.

095 suggest
[səgdʒést]

v. 암시하다, 제의하다
show an idea or feeling without stating it directly; mention an idea, possible plan or action for other people

syn **indicate** 나타내다, 지시하다 **propose, advocate** 제안하다 **hint, imply** 암시하다

The report suggested various ways in which the service could be improved.
그 보고서에는 서비스를 개선할 수 있는 다양한 방법이 언급되어 있었다.

Word Root	▸ voc, vok = call
convoke	v. [회의를] 소집하다
equivocal	a. 이중 의미의, 애매한 [equ=same]
evoke	v. [법에] 호소하다, 영혼을 불러내다
irrevocable	a. 최종적인, 철회할 수 없는
provoke	v. 성나게 하다, 도발하다
revoke	v. [명령, 동의, 허가를] 철회[취소]하다 [re=back]
vocation	n. 직업(옛날에는 하늘이 부른 것을 천직이라 했다)

096 bear
[bɛər]

v. 낳다, 참다, 나르다
give birth to; put up with; contain or hold

syn **produce, yield** 낳다, 산출하다 **stand, tolerate** 참다 **carry** 나르다

She bore three sons 30 years ago, but two of them died in the battlefield.
그녀는 30년 전에 아들을 셋 낳았으나 둘은 전장에서 죽고 말았다.

Plus Data
bear - bore - born 낳다
bore - bored - bored 구멍을 뚫다

097 intact
[intækt]

a. 손상되지 않은, 영향받지 않은, 그대로의
not damaged; complete and in the original state

syn undamaged, unimpaired, unchanged, unaltered, untouched 손상되지 않은, 그대로의

His image as a party leader has survived the crisis intact
그 위기에도 불구하고 정당 지도자로서의 그의 위상은 실추되지 않았다.

---

098 **bold**
[bould]

a. 용감한, 대담한
fearless and daring

syn valiant, brave, courageous, audacious, fearless, daring 용감한, 대담한

The engineer had a bold plan to build a bridge over the English Channel.
그 기술자는 영국 해협 위로 다리를 놓는 대담한 계획을 세웠다.

> **Plus Data**
> bald a. 대머리의, 꾸밈없는

---

099 **initial**
[iníʃəl]

a. 처음의
occurring at the beginning

syn first, original 처음의, 최초의

At the initial stage of the project not everyone had access to a computer.
그 프로젝트의 첫 단계 때에는 모든 구성원이 컴퓨터를 쓸 수 있었던 것은 아니었다.

initially ad. 최초로 syn. originally
initiate v. 시작하다 syn. begin, start, commence, originate, launch, take off

---

100 **whereas**
[hwὲəræz]

conj. ~에 반해서
compared with the fact that

syn on the contrary 반면에 while, since ~인 까닭에

Doctors salaries have risen substantially, whereas nurses pay has actually fallen.
의사의 봉급은 상당히 오른 반면, 간호사의 월급은 사실상 내렸다.

---

101 **blot out**

v. 감추다, 빛을 가리다
make imperceptible by concealing; hide or block the light from something

[syn] **cover, hide, conceal** 감추다

Dark clouds overhead had blotted out the sun.
머리 위의 먹구름이 태양을 가려버렸다.

102 **capture**
[kǽptʃər]

v. 표현하다, 포착하다
succeed in representing something using words or images

[syn] **catch, seize, record** 잡다, 녹화하다

Most of the men had been either killed or captured.
그 사람들은 대부분 죽임을 당하거나 사로잡혔다.

103 **cluster**
[klʌ́stər]

n. 묶음
a group of similar things

v. 모이다
gather into a cluster

[syn] **group, batch** 한 묶음 | **concentrate, assemble, converge, flock, gather, swarm** 모이다, 밀집하다

People stood in clusters around the notice boards.
사람들이 게시판 주변에 삼삼오오 모여 있었다.

104 **obtain**
[əbtéin]

v. 얻다, 획득하다
come into possession of

[syn] **achieve, attain, gain, acquire, capture, grasp** 성취하다, 얻다

Hunting license must be obtained in some national parks.
일부 국립공원에서는 사냥 허가증을 구입해야 한다.

105 **alter**
[ɔ́:ltər]

v. 바꾸다
cause to change; make different

[syn] **change, modify** 변경하다, 수정하다

The recent changes in the facade altered the overall impression of the building.
최근에 건물의 앞면을 고쳤더니 건물의 전체적인 분위기가 바뀌었다.

Plus Data
altar n. 제단

106 remarkable
[rimá:rkəbl]

a. 주목할 만한, 두드러진
unusual or striking and worth mentioning

syn **notable, extraordinary, exceptional, incredible**
두드러진, 특별한, 믿을 수 없는

Students in the test group displayed remarkable growth in their performance. 실험 집단의 학생들이 두드러진 성적 향상을 보였다.

107 vivid
[vívid]

a. 생생한, 생기 있는
producing very clear and detailed images in mind; animated

syn **graphic, bright, live** 생생한, 활기찬, 살아 있는

I've been having extraordinarily vivid dreams recently.
최근 나는 범상치 않은, 생생한 꿈을 꾸곤 한다.

108 deliberate
[dilíbərət]

a. 심사숙고한, 고의적인
carefully thought out in advance; planned

syn **thoughtful** 사려 깊은 **prudent, discreet, careful**
신중한 **intentional** 의도적인

I'm sure the omission of my name was deliberate.
내 이름을 고의로 빼먹은 게 분명해.

109 depict
[dipíkt]

v. 묘사하다
give a description of

syn **picture, describe, represent** 묘사하다, 나타내다

In these days, a television drama depicting the life of the artist is the rage. 요즘 그 예술가의 삶을 그리는 텔레비전 드라마가 유행이다.
*be the rage 유행이다

110 create
[kriéit]

v. 창조하다
bring into existence; make to be or to become

syn **produce, invent, make** 만들다

In the last week, 170 new jobs have been created.
지난 주에 170개의 새로운 일자리가 창출되었다.

111 employ
[implɔ́i]

v. 고용하다
hire for work

syn **use, utilize** 사용하다 **hire** 고용하다

Two procedures can be employed to test this particular hypothesis. 이 가설을 실험해 보는 데 두 가지 방법이 사용될 수 있다.

Word Root ▶ plic, ply = fold

apply	v. 신청하다
applicable	a. 적용할 수 있는, 적절한
complicate	v. 복잡하게 하다
explicate	v. [상세히] 설명하다 [ex=out]
imply	v. 함축하다
implicate	v. [사건, 범죄에] 관련되다
implicit	a. 은밀한, 함축적인
simplicity	n. 단순, 간단

---

112 transformation
[trænsfərméiʃən]

n. 변형, 변화

the act or instance of changing appearance or nature;
the state of being transformed

syn **conversion, modification, change** 전환, 변형, 변화

Nixon's visit led to a transformation of American attitudes toward China. 닉슨의 방문으로 중국에 대한 미국인의 태도가 바뀌었다.

Word Root ▶ form = norm

conform	v. (to) 순응시키다
deform	v. 모양을 망치다
inform	v. ~에게 알리다
perform	v. 실행[이행]하다
reform	v. 개혁하다

---

113 alternative
[ɔːltə́ːrnətiv]

n. 양자 택일, 대안

one of two or more things to be chosen; something which can be chosen instead

syn **choice, option** 선택, 대안 **rotation** 교대

There was no alternative but to close the road until February. 2월까지 도로를 차단하는 길밖에는 다른 대안이 없었다.

alternate a. 다른, 선택적인 syn. other, another, selective

alter v. 바꾸다, 교대하다 syn. change, interchange, rotate, recur

---

114 cede
[siːd]

v. 양보하다

give something unwillingly

syn **yield, relinquish, surrender, give up, abandon**
양보하다, 포기하다

Mexico ceded New Mexico to the United States in 1848.
멕시코는 1848년 미국에 뉴멕시코 주를 이양했다.

ceding n. 양보 syn. yielding

115 **yield**
[ji:ld]

v. (결과 · 이익을) 가져오다
be the cause or source of

syn **produce, provide** 생산하다, 공급하다 **surrender, give up** 포기하다

Knowing about our past does not automatically yield solutions to our current problems. 우리의 과거를 안다고 해서 우리가 안고 있는 현 문제점들에 대한 해결책이 나오지는 않는다.

116 **assemble**
[əsémbl]

v. ① 조립하다, 모으다
make by putting pieces together; collect in one place
② 모이다
come together

syn **gather, bring together, put together, collect, congregate** 모이다, 모으다

The children assembled outside the building.
아이들이 건물 밖에 모였다.

117 **immense**
[iméns]

a. 광대한, 거대한, 막대한
unusually great in size, amount, degree, extent, or scope

syn **large, enormous, vast, huge, massive, ample, stupendous, grand, great** 거대한, 굉장한

The pressure on students during exam time can be immense. 시험 기간 동안 학생들에게 가해지는 압박감은 굉장하다.

118 **magnify**
[mǽgnəfài]

v. 확대하다
make large; increase in size, volume, or significance

syn **increase, amplify, intensify** 확대하다, 강화하다

Bacteria are magnified to 1,000 times their actual size through the microscope.
현미경을 통해 박테리아를 보면 실제 크기의 1000배로 확대된다.

119 **constrain**
[kənstréin]

v. 강요하다, 억제하다
control and limit something; hold back

[syn] **bound, restrict, limit, control, check** 제한하다, 막다

The fundamental problems of early apartment buildings in New York are that they are constrained to 25 by 100 feet rectangular shaped ground lot. 초기에 지어진 뉴욕의 아파트 빌딩들이 갖고 있는 근본 문제는 부지가 25×100평방 피트로 제한되어 있다는 점이다.

constrained a. 제한된 syn. restricted

120 **administer**
[ædmínistər]

v. 관리하다
manage or govern

[syn] **manage, govern, execute** 관리하다, 집행하다

The foundation was formed specifically to administer the project. 그 프로젝트를 집행하기 위한 특별 기금이 조성되었다.

administered a. 관리된, 주어진 syn. given

Review

□ create _____

□ remarkable _____

□ subsidize _____

□ deliberate _____

□ suggest _____

□ bear _____

□ administer _____

□ bold _____

□ depict _____

□ transformation _____

□ blot out _____

□ cede _____

□ magnify _____

□ constrain _____

□ alter _____

□ assemble _____

□ vivid _____

□ whereas _____

□ rigorous _____

□ generate _____

□ employ _____

□ initial _____

□ alternative _____

□ obtain _____

□ yield _____

□ celebrated _____

□ immense _____

□ cluster _____

□ intact _____

□ capture _____

121-150

121 assert
[əsə́ːrt]

v. 단언하다, 주장하다
state clearly or firmly; announce officially

syn **declare, profess, claim, insist, affirm, aver, argue, contend** 선언하다, 단언하다, 주장하다, 논쟁하다

The defendant asserted his innocence.
피고는 자신의 무죄를 주장했다.

122 acquire
[əkwàiər]

v. 얻다
come into the possession of something concrete or abstract

syn **obtain, get** 얻다

Bruce Green acquired the company for 100 million dollars.
브루스 그린은 그 회사를 1억 달러에 인수했다.

acquired a. 후천적인, 습득된(↔ natural 선천적인)

Plus Data
acquire through, gain from ~을 통해 얻다

123 achieve
[ətʃíːv]

v. 이루다, 얻다
carry out successfully; gain with effort

syn **accomplish, carry out, attain** 이루다, 얻다

The Republic of Tunisia achieved independence from France in 1957. 튀니지 공화국은 1957년 프랑스로부터 독립을 얻어냈다.

124 agrarian
[əgrɛ́əriən]

a. 농민의, 토지의, 농업의
relating to or characteristic of farmers or their life; relating to the land and cultivation

syn **relating to or involving farming or farmers**
농지의, 농업의, 농민의

Government had to make a new agrarian project in order to compensate for the lost crops because of severe draught last summer. 정부는 지난 여름 심한 가뭄 때문에 손실을 입은

곡물을 보충하기 위해 새로운 농업 정책을 수립해야 했다.

Plus Data
agriculture n. 농업   syn. farming

125 **serene**
[sərí:n]

a. 조용한, [마음이] 평화로운, 화창한
peaceful and calm; completely clear and fine

syn **calm, peaceful, tranquil, silent, still, quiet**
고요한, 조용한

There were no cars in this street and thus the neighborhood was very serene.
이 거리에는 차가 안 다녀서 동네가 아주 조용했다.

126 **vast**
[væst]

a. 거대한, 광대한
unusually great in size, amount, degree, or extent

syn **great, enormous, huge, immense** 거대한

The elephants at the zoo eat a vast amount of food each day. 그 동물원에 있는 코끼리들은 매일 엄청난 양의 먹이를 먹는다.

127 **emit**
[imít]

v. [빛, 열 등을] 내뿜다
give off light, heat, or radiation

syn **give off, exhale, release** 발산하다, 방출하다

Stars emit radiation. 별들은 복사 에너지를 방출한다.

128 **duplicate**
[djú:plikət]

v. 복제하다
make an exact copy of something
a. 중복의, 똑같은, 복제의
being an exact copy of something

syn **imitate, copy, reproduce, clone** 모방하다, 복제하다 | **identical, equal, equivalent, same** 동일한

Digital images can be duplicated in seconds.
디지털 영상은 몇 초 만에 복제가 가능하다.

129 **feasible**
[fí:zəbl]

a. 실행할 수 있는, 가능한, 그럴듯한
able to be done or achieved; possible or reasonable

syn **possible** 가능한 **plausible** 그럴듯한 **physical, real,**

virtual, actual, practical 실제적인

There seems to be only one feasible solution.
한 가지 해결책만이 실행 가능해 보인다.

---

130 **hub**
[hʌb]

n. 중심
the central part of something

[syn] **center, central spot, core, heart** 중심 **focus** 초점

Bombay is the financial hub of India.
봄베이는 인도의 금융 거점이다.

---

131 **although**
[ɔːlðóu]

conj. 비록 ~이지만
despite the fact that

[syn] **though, even though, but, even if, while**
비록 ~이지만

Although it does not rain much, Travis county suffers much from frequent flood because of its non-permeable land layer. 트래비스 카운티에는 비가 많이 오지는 않지만 지층이 물을 흡수하지 못해 잦은 홍수로 고통을 겪는다.

---

132 **exhibit**
[igzíbit]

v. 공개하다, 보여주다
show something public; show an attribute or property

[syn] **feature, present, show, display** 특징을 그리다, 보여주다

His work has been exhibited regularly at the Walker Art Gallery. 그의 작품은 Walker Art Gallery에서 정기적으로 전시되어 왔다.

Word Root	▶ hab, hib = live
habitual	a. 습관의, 버릇이 된
habitat	n. [동식물의] 산지, 서식지
inhabitant	n. 거주자, 서식 동물
inhibit	v. 방해하다, 억제하다 [in=not]
prohibit	n. 금지하다

---

133 **accumulate**
[əkjúːmjulèit]

v. 축적하다, 축적되다
collect over a long time; gradually increase in number or amount

[syn] **collect, build up, amass, gather, hoard, store**

모으다, 축적하다, 저장하다

Over the years, the collector had accumulated hundreds of books. 몇 년에 걸쳐 그 장서가는 수백 권의 책을 모았다.

134 appeal
[əpíːl]

v. 간청하다, 호감을 사다
request earnestly; be attractive to

n. 간청, 매력
earnest or urgent request; attractiveness

syn entreat, implore, plead, request, attract 간청하다, 유혹하다 | entreaty, petition, plea, request 간청, 탄원

The heavily flooded region appealed to the whole country for help. 크게 홍수 피해를 입은 지역에서 전국적인 도움을 호소했다.

Word Root	▶ pel, puls = drive
compel	v. 억지로 ~을 시키다
compulsory	a. 의무적인
dispel	v. [불길한 생각을] 쫓아버리다, 분산시키다
expel	v. 내쫓다
impel	v. 추진시키다
impulse	n. 추진[력]
propel	v. 추진하다
repel	v. 쫓아버리다, 불쾌감을 일으키다
repulse	v. 쫓아버리다
repellent	a. 불쾌한

135 migrate
[màigreit]

v. 이주하다
to move one place to another

syn travel, shift, move long distance from one place to another 이주하다

Blue whales and reindeers are two exemplary animal groups that migrate.
먼 거리를 이동해 다니는 동물의 예로 흰수염고래와 순록, 두 동물을 들 수 있다.

Plus Data
immigrate 이주해 들어오다 ↔ emigrate 이민을 나가다

136 mimic
[mímik]

v. 흉내내다
imitate a person, a manner, etc.

syn imitate, copy, mirror 흉내내다

The company has computers with the ability to mimic

human intelligence.
그 회사는 사람의 지능을 흉내낼 수 있는 컴퓨터를 보유하고 있다.

137 **component**
[kəmpóunənt]

n. 구성 요소
a constituent

syn **element, ingredient, constituent, member, part** 요소, 성분, 구성 요소, 부분

Try breaking the problem down into its separate
components. 그 문제를 분석해서 세부 각론으로 나눠 보아라.

138 **inhabit**
[inhǽbit]

v. 거주하다, 서식하다
live in a place; make one's home

syn **live in, reside, dwell, occupy** 거주하다

Five thousand people inhabit the small island.
5,000명의 인구가 그 조그만 섬에 거주한다.

inhabitant n. 거주자 syn. resident, citizen, denizen, tenant,
occupant

Plus Data
inhibit v. 막다, 구속하다 syn. bridle, constrain, curb, obstruct, restrain,
restrict, control, check, limit

139 **attract**
[ətrǽkt]

v. 매혹하다
draw toward oneself or itself

syn **appeal, tempt, allure, draw, charm** 매혹하다, 끌다

The show attracts viewers from every sector of society.
사회 각층의 사람들이 그 공연을 보러 온다.

140 **comprise**
[kəmpràiz]

v. 구성되다, 포함하다
be composed of; have as a component

syn **consist of, make up of, constitute, contain, embrace, encompass, include** 구성되다, 포함하다

The committee is comprised of representatives from both
the public and private sectors.
그 위원회는 공공 부문과 민간 부문 대표자 모두를 포함한다.

comprising a.구성하는 syn. including

141 capability
[kèipəbíləti]

n. 능력, 가능성
the quality of being capable physically, intellectually, or legally

syn **ability, competence** 능력 **proficiency** 숙달, 능숙 **aptitude** 소질 **faculty, skill, talent** 재능, 재주 **potential** 가능성

Only pilots of the highest capability are chosen to become test pilots. 최정예 파일럿만이 시험 비행에 선발될 수 있다.

142 mark
[mɑːrk]

v. 눈에 띄다, 표시하다, 인지하다
be a distinctive feature; make or leave a mark on; notice

syn **indicate** 지시하다, 나타내다

The two players are markedly different in their style of play. 그 두 선수의 플레이 방식은 현저하게 다르다.

marked a. 분명한 syn. obvious, noticeable, conspicuous, evident, pronounced

143 avail
[əvéil]

n. 이익, 유용성
use, purpose, advantage, or profit
v. 도움이 되다, 이롭다
be of use or advantage to

syn **use, advantage** 쓸모, 이익 | **use, utilize, make use of, take advantage of** 이용하다

Words of encouragement were to no avail to Frida Gallo. 어떤 격려의 말도 프리다 갈로에게는 소용이 없었다.

available a. 가용한, 쓸모 있는 syn. accessible, obtainable, convenient

avail oneself of ~ 이용하다, 틈타다(use something to one's advantage or benefit)

144 associate
[əsóuʃièit]

v. 관련시키다, 교제하다
make a logical or casual connection; keep company with

syn **relate, connect** 관련시키다, 연관시키다

While Amy Beckett was in Paris, she associated with many well-known artists.
에이미 베케트는 파리에 체류하는 동안 저명한 많은 예술가들과 어울렸다.

145 accessible
[æksésəbl]

a. 얻기 쉬운, [사람, 장소가] 접근하기 쉬운
able to be reached or easily obtained; easy to get along

syn **reachable, available, obtainable** 얻기 쉬운

The community leader's goal was to make adult education more accessible. 그 지역 지도자의 목표는 성인 교육의 기회를 좀 더 쉽게 접할 수 있도록 하는 것이었다.

146 deplete
[diplí:t]

v. 고갈시키다, 감소시키다
use up, as of resources or materials; reduce something, esp. of energy, money or similar

syn **use up, exhaust, run out, consume, devour, expend, spend** 고갈시키다, 다 써버리다

Wars in the region have depleted the country's food supplies. 그 지역의 전쟁은 전국의 식량을 고갈시켰다.

147 largely
[lá:rdʒli]

ad. 대부분, 주로
almost completely

syn **mostly, generally** 대체로, 일반적으로

The research findings are largely due to recent development in the instruments employed in the project. 연구 성과는 그 프로젝트에 사용된 최신 기기들의 기여가 컸다.

148 diverse
[divə́:rs]

a. 다양한, 다른
varied or different

syn **various, assorted, different, dissimilar** 다양한, 다른

The newspaper aims to cover a diverse range of issues. 그 신문은 다양한 범주의 이슈를 다루고자 한다.

diversity n. 다양함 syn. variety, difference, divergence

149 avid
[ǽvid]

a. 열정적인
marked by active interest and enthusiasm

syn **enthusiastic, highly desirous, ardent, eager, passionate, energetic** 열정적인

Diane Schallert was an avid reader; she read all kinds of books within her reach.
다이앤 셸러트는 독서광이었다. 그녀는 손에 잡히는 대로 책을 읽어댔다.

150 **bound**
[baund]

a. 의무가 있는, 강요된, 묶인

being under moral or legal obligation; tied

syn **fastened, tied, constrained, compelled, obligated** 묶인, 제한된, 강요된

The tenant is bound by the contract to pay the rent before the end of the month.

세입자는 계약에 따라 월말이 되기 전에 집세를 지불해야 한다.

Review

□ capability _____

□ mimic _____

□ avail _____

□ bound _____

□ largely _____

□ comprise _____

□ accessible _____

□ emit _____

□ deplete _____

□ avid _____

□ diverse _____

□ mark _____

□ accumulate _____

□ appeal _____

□ inhabit _____

□ acquire _____

□ component _____

□ migrate _____

□ attract _____

□ vast _____

□ assert _____

□ hub _____

□ achieve _____

□ associate _____

□ duplicate _____

□ feasible _____

□ serene _____

□ although _____

□ exhibit _____

□ agrarian _____

Weekend

인문 I 역사, 정치, 경제, 사회, 예술

U.S Social History
역사, 정치, 경제, 사회

독립전쟁

puritan 청교도

migrate 이주하다

settlement 정착지, 거처

colonization 식민지화

annex (영토를) 병합하다

American revolution 미국독립전쟁

Declaration of independence 독립선언서

남북전쟁

Civil War 남북전쟁

Emancipation Proclamation 노예해방선언

Federal government 연방정부

ranch 목장

pasture 목초지

plantation 고무, 면화, 사탕수수 등을 재배하는 대규모 농장

slavery 노예제도

Union 북군

Confederacy 남부연합

사법제도

judicial 사법의

The U.S. Constitution 미국 헌법

unconstitutional 위헌의

Supreme Court 대법원

circuit court 순회 재판소

trial 재판, 소송

case 사건, 사례

party (소송의) 당사자

plaintiff 원고, 고발인

defendant 피고

jury 배심원

amnesty 사면

의회제도

legislative 입법의

amendment 수정, 개정

liberalization 법률, 규칙의 완화

provision 조항, 규정

Capitol 미국 국회의사당

Congress 미국 의회

political party 정당

Senate 상원

House of Representative 하원

opposition leader 야당 원내총무

electoral college 선거인단

prerogative 특권

radical 과격한, 극단적인

행정제도

administrative 행정의(=executive)

executive office 행정부

Cabinet 내각

Oval Office 대통령 집무실

veto 거부권

ratify 비준하다, 인가하다

public hearing 공청회

public servant 공무원

bureaucratic 관료적인

check and balances 견제와 균형

prohibition 금주법

institution 제도, 관습

경제

Great Depression 대공황

New Deal 뉴딜 정책

taxpayer 납세자

patent 특허

사회

civil rights 시민권

Civil Rights Act 공민권법

racial discrimination 인종 차별

integration 인종 차별 폐지

segregation 격리, 인종 차별

minority 소수민족

doctrine 교리, 주의

Indian Reservation 인디언 거류지

Art History

예술사

abstractionism 추상주의

aesthetic 미학의

Art Deco 아르데코(1920~30년대 장식 양식)

Art Nouveau 아르누보(미술디자인 양식)

avant-garde 전위, 선봉

azure 하늘색

brush stroke 붓칠

brushwork 화풍, 화법

caricature 풍자화

chiaroscuro 명암법

chromatic 색채의

composition 구도

connoisseur 전문가, 감정가

constriction of space 공간의 축소

contour line 윤곽선

copperplate print 동판화

Cubism 입체파

Dadaism 다다이즘(surrealism의 근간이 됨)

deformation 변형

emboss 돋을 새김으로 하다(양각으로 하다)

engraving 조각술, 판화

Environment Art 환경예술

etching 부식 동판술

Expressionism 표현주의(주관을 극도로 강조하는 유파)

Fauvism 야수파

formative arts 조형미술

fresco 프레스코 화법

Futurism 미래파(인습을 타파하고 새로운 국면을 개척하려고 1910년경 이탈리아에서 일어난 미술, 음악, 문화의 유파)

Gothic 고딕 양식의

hue 색조

illustrate 삽화를 넣다, 예증하다

impressionism 인상주의

limpid 투명한

lithograph 석판화

lucent 빛나는, 반투명의

luster 광택

monochrome 단색화

opaque 불투명한

pigment 안료

plaster cast 석고상

Pointillism 점묘법

pop art 팝아트

portrait 초상화, 인물화

Post-impressionism 후기인상주의

Post-Modernism 포스트모더니즘

profile 측면도

rendering 표현

reproduction 복제

realism 사실주의

relief 부조 양각

Renaissance 문예 부흥기

Rococo 로코코 양식

still-life painting 정물화

Surrealism 초현실주의

Symbolism 상징주의

tempera 템페라 화법(유화의 초기 형태)

theatrical 연극의

vandalism 문화예술의 파괴주의

vantage point 관점

washes 담채화

watercolor 수채물감

wood point 목판화

Literature

문학

abridge 요약하다

allegory 우화, 비유

alliteration 두운(법)

allusion 암시

annotation 주석

anonymous 익명의

anthology 시선집, 전집

archaic 고어체의

archetype 전형

authenticity 출처가 분명함

authorship 원작자임

bibliography 서지학, 출판, 참고 서적 목록

catharsis 카타르시스

censorship 검열

character 인물

chronicle 연대기

civilized 문명화 된

cliché 진부한 표현

colloquial 구어의

commentator 주석자

compendium 개요

cynicism 냉소주의

decadence 타락, 퇴폐

deconstruction 해체

denouement 대단원

dialectic 변증법

dialects 방언

draft 초안

elegy 애가, 비가

ellipsis 생략, 생략 부호

empiricism 경험주의

epic 서사시

epigram 경구

epitome 요약

eulogy 찬사, 칭송

excerpt 인용구, 발췌

existentialism 실존주의

folklore 민속학

innuendo 암시, 풍자

irony 풍자, 반어

lyric 서정시의

materialism 유물론

metaphor 은유

metaphysical 형이상학의

paradox 역설

paraphrase 바꿔 쓰기

parody 패러디(일종의 문학적 인용)

piracy 표절("해적질"이라는 원래의 뜻에서 변화됨)

pirate 저작권 침해자("해적"이라는 원래의 뜻에서 변화됨)

plagiarize 표절하다

plot 구성

prose 산문

protagonist 소설의 주인공

pseudonym 가명

rhetoric 수사법

satire 풍자, 풍자문학

stereotype 고정관념, 판에 박힌 문구

style 문체

structuralism 구조주의

stylist 문장가

subscribe 잡지를 구독하다

terse (문체,표현이) 간결한

theme 주제

version 번역

wit 위트, 재치

Music

음악

accompaniment 반주

ad lib 즉흥 연주

arrangement 편곡

beat 박자

chamber music 실내악

chromatic 반음계의

clef 음자리표

compose 작곡하다

composition (음악) 작곡

conductor 지휘자

enthusiasm 열정

syncopation 절분음, 당김음

improvisation 즉흥 연주

intonation 음조, 곡조

inventiveness 독창성

march 행진곡

measure 소절, meter 박자

movement 악장

a national anthem 국가

note 음표, 음조

piece 작품

pluck (현악기) 타다, 잡아뜯다

polyphony 다성음악

scale 음계

score 악보

string 현악기

tone 음색

tune 곡조

variation 편곡, 변주

Film

영화

adaptation 각색

avant-garde 전위의

cinematic 영화의

close-up 근접 촬영

commentary 논쟁, 논평

critical 비평가의

documentary 기록영화

dramatist 극작가

dramatize 극화 하다

echo 흉내 내다, 반향하다

formalism 구성주의, 형식주의

montage 몽타주

realism 사실주의

2nd week

151-180

151 **ooze**
[u:z]

v. 스며나오다
flow slowly out of something through a small opening

syn **flow slowly, move slowly** 천천히 흐르다, 움직이다 |
disclosure 폭로 **mud** 진흙
The cut on the tree was oozing sap.
나무의 절단면에서 수액이 흘러나왔다.

oozing a. 흘러나오는 syn. exuding, trickling, flowing

152 **prestige**
[prestí:dʒ]

n. 명성, 위세
a high standing achieved through success or wealth

syn **honor, fame, status** 명예, 유명함, 지위

The movie was designed to enhance the author's personal
prestige. 그 영화는 작가 개인의 명성을 부각시키기 위해 제작되었다.

153 **outstanding**
[àutstǽndiŋ]

a. 뛰어난, 두드러진
distinguished from others in excellence

syn **prominent, eminent, remarkable** 두드러진, 뛰어난
famous 유명한
Making a traditional basket is an outstanding example of
Indian art. 전통 바구니 제작 기술은 뛰어난 인디언 수공예의 한 예이다.

154 **barter**
[bá:rtər]

v. 물물 교환하다
exchange goods without involving money

syn **exchange, swap, trade** 교환하다, 물물 교환하다, 거래하다
The people in the village got what they needed by bartering
their livestock. 마을 사람들은 가축을 교환함으로써 그들이 필요한 것을 얻었다.

barter system 물물 교환

Plus Data
swab v. 물기를 닦다

155 hearten
[háːrtn]

v. 용기를 북돋워주다
give encouragement to

syn cheer up, encourage 용기를 북돋워주다

The candidate was heartened by the public's support.
후보자는 대중의 지지로 용기를 얻었다.

156 mode
[moud]

n. [일·문제 처리 등의] 특정 상태, 방법, 양식, 유행
a particular functioning condition or arrangement; a way of operating, living, or behaving; the current fashion

syn form, method, fashion, scale 형태(방식), 방법, 유행, 음계

The spacecraft was in its recovery mode.
우주비행선은 회복 모드(단계)에 있었다.

157 tailor
[téilər]

v. [요구·조건에 맞도록] 조절하다
make fit for a specific purpose

syn adapt, fit, modify 조절하다, 알맞게 하다, 변경하다

All the courses provided in the college can be tailored to the needs of individuals.
대학에서 제공되는 모든 교과 과정은 개개인의 필요에 따라 조절될 수 있다.

tailored a. 맞춰진 syn. adapted

Plus Data
tailor-made clothes 맞춤복 syn. custom clothes

158 shift
[ʃift]

v. 이동하다
change place or direction slightly
n. [위치·방향의] 이동, 변화
a change in position or direction

syn move, transfer, change 이동하다 | alteration, direction [위치·방향의] 이동, 변화

Public opinion had shifted sharply following the war.
여론은 전쟁 후에 급격히 변해갔다.

159 **simultaneous**
[sàiməltéiniəs]

a. 동시에 일어나는
occurring or operating at the same time

syn **concurrent, synchronized, concomitant** 동시에 일어나는, 동반하는, 수반하는

In simultaneous announcements, the two men resigned from their jobs. 동시 발표로 그 두 사람이 사직했다.

simultaneously ad. 동시에 syn. at the same time

160 **staple**
[stéipl]

n. 기본 식료품, 중요 상품, 주요 산물
necessary foods or commodities

a. 기본적인, 주요한
basic or main

syn **basic element, ingredient** 구성 요소 | **important, chief, major, primary** 중요한, 주요한

The shops are running out of staples such as rice and cooking oil. 상점에는 쌀과 식용유 같은 필수품이 떨어지고 있다.

161 **stem from**

v. 유래하다, 생기다
have roots in, originate in, grow out of

syn **result from, arise from, derive from, grow out of** 유래하다

Many of current problems of the society stem from its adherence to seemingly outdated customs.
사회에서 현재 벌어지고 있는 많은 문제들은 시대에 뒤떨어져 보이는 관습들을 고수하려는 데서 비롯되고 있다.

162 **random**
[rǽndəm]

a. 무작위의
happening; done or chosen by chance

syn **casual, unsystematic, without planning** 우연의, 비조직적인, 무계획의

The computer will generate random numbers for lottery tickets. 컴퓨터는 복권을 위한 무작위 수를 만들어 낼 것이다.

Plus Data
by chance 우연히

163 rare
[rɛər]

a. 드문
not common, not widely distributed

syn **unusual, scarce, infrequent, uncommon, unique, exceptional** 드문

It's extremely rare for the arbiter to lose her temper.
중재하는 사람이 화를 내는 것은 아주 드문 일이다.

rarely ad. 거의 ~않는   syn. barely, scarcely, hardly, seldom

164 hollow
[hálou]

a. 속이 빈
having a space or gap

n. 구멍, 움푹한 곳
a hole or empty space in something; a low area in a surface

syn **empty, void, vacant, unoccupied** 빈, 점유되지 않은 | **an empty space** 빈 공간

The dried out tree trunk was completely hollow.
마른 나무 줄기는 완전히 비어 있었다.

165 impair
[impɛ́ər]

v. 손상시키다
spoil; make worse or less effective

syn **injure, damage, weaken** 손상시키다, 약화시키다

The condition of the candidate does not seem to impair his ability to work.
후보자의 조건은 그의 업무 수행 능력에 흠을 내지는 않는 것 같다.

166 novel
[návəl]

a. 새로운
of a kind not seen before

syn **unusual, strange, new** 비범한, 이상한, 새로운

The engineers tried to find a novel solution to the problem.
기술자들은 그 문제의 새로운 해결책을 찾으려고 노력했다.

167 encompass
[inkʌ́mpəs]

v. 포함하다, 둘러싸다
include a variety of things

syn **include, contain, surround** 포함하다

The student debates will encompass a range of subjects.
학생 토론은 다양한 주제를 두루 다룰 것이다.

168 flaw
[flɔ:]

n. 결점

defect or weakness in a person's character; an imperfection in a device or machine

syn **defect, weakness, drawback** 결점, 단점 **problem, error** 문제

There are serious flaws in the way the teachers are trained.
교사들을 육성하는 방식에 중대한 결점들이 있다.

flawless a. 흠이 없는 syn. perfect, absolute, uncut

Plus Data
merit(↔ flaw) n. 장점 syn. strength

169 hence
[hens]

ad. 결과적으로, 지금부터

from that fact or reason; from this time

syn **accordingly, consequently, therefore** 따라서, 결과적으로, 그러므로

Crime is on the increase, hence the need for more police.
범죄가 늘어나고 있다. 이에 따라 경찰에 대한 수요도 늘고 있다.

170 derive
[diràiv]

v. [본원·원천에서] ~을 얻다, 유래하다

obtain; develop or evolve from

syn **obtain, gain** 얻다 **stem from, originate** 유래하다

There are many products that are derived from animals.
동물로부터 얻는 생산물이 많이 있다.

171 vex
[veks]

v. 성가시게 하다, 괴롭히다

cause annoyance, disturb, or difficulty

syn **make difficult** 난처하게 하다 **annoy, irritate** 성나게 하다

Nothing vexes Teresa more than the constant comparison with her rival Joan Anderson. 그녀의 경쟁자인 조앤 앤더슨과 끊임없이 비교하는 것처럼 테레사를 화나게 하는 것은 없다.

vexing a. 어려운, 성가신 syn. difficult, troublesome

172 vulnerable
[vʌ́lnərəbl]

a. 상처받기 쉬운

susceptible to physical or emotional injury

syn **easily to be damaged** 상처받기 쉬운 **susceptible**

[영향을] 받기 쉬운 **weak** 약한 **defenseless, exposed, accessible** 무방비의

The government must help the most vulnerable groups in our society. 정부는 우리 사회에서 가장 약한 집단을 도와야만 한다.

173 **ultimately**
[ˈʌltəmətli]

ad. 결국, 궁극적으로
as the end result of a process; after everything has been considered

syn **eventually, finally** 결국에는 **primarily** 근본적으로, 우선

The researchers efforts to create a new plant species ultimately failed after a long period of trials.
새로운 식물종 창조에 관한 연구원들의 노력은 오랜 시도 끝에 결국에는 실패하였다.

174 **subside**
[səbsàid]

v. 가라앉다, 진정되다
become less strong; wear off; die down

syn **diminish, lessen, become less, shrink, contracts, fall down** 감소하다, 줄어들다, 누그러지다

By morning, the storm had subsided.
아침이 되자 폭풍은 누그러져 있었다.

subsided a. 줄어든 syn. diminished, reduced

Plus Data
subsidy n. 자금 syn. funding, financing

175 **sequent**
[síːkwənt]

a. 연속하는, 결과로서 생기는
happening after something else; following as an effect or result

syn **successive** 연속하는, 계속적인 **following** 다음에 오는 **later** 뒤의

A computer can store and repeat sequences of instructions.
컴퓨터는 연속된 지시들을 반복하고 저장할 수 있다.

sequence n. 연속, 계속 syn. series, arrangement, order, progression, succession

Plus Data
consequence n. 결과, 중요성 syn. results, importance, significance

176 **promising**
[prάmisiŋ]

a. 가능성 있는
showing possibility of achievement or excellence

syn **potential, hopeful** 잠재력이 있는, 유망한

We are entering a promising era in narcolepsy research.
우리는 나르콜렙시 연구 분야에서 전망이 밝은 시대에 돌입하고 있다.

* narcolepsy (간질병의) 기면발작, 나르콜렙시

177 **pledge**
[pledʒ]

n. 서약, 보증
a binding commitment to do or give or refrain from something

v. 서약하다
make a serious formal promise to give or to do

syn **appointment** 약속 **guarantee, warranty** 보증 |
promise 서약하다 **swear, vow** 맹세하다

Sunday's vote was a test of the new president's pledge
of fair elections.
일요일의 투표는 새 대통령의 공정선거 서약에 대한 시험대였다.

178 **pore**
[pɔːr]

v. 숙고하다
focus one's attention on something

n. [피부의] 털구멍
any small opening in the skin

syn **examine, ponder, review** 숙고하다 | **hole, opening,
crevice, gap** 구멍, 틈

He pored over the classified ads in search of a new job.
그는 새로운 일자리를 구하기 위해 신문 구인란을 자세히 들여다보았다.

179 **persist**
[pərsíst]

v. 지속하다, 고집하다
continue to exist; refuse to stop

syn **endure, remain, keep on, insist** 지속하다

Two families have old hostilities that have persisted for
years. 두 집안은 오랫동안 지속되어 온 적개심을 가지고 있다.

Word Root	▸ sist = stand
assist	v. 돕다, 공헌하다
consist	v. ~으로 이루어지다
desist	v. 그만두다, 중지하다
insist	v. 주장하다
subsist	v. 생존하다, 살아가다
resist	v. 저항하다, 반대하다

180 **liken**
[làikən]

v. 비유하다, 닮게 하다
consider or describe as similar or equal

syn **compare, equate** 비유하다, 동일시하다

Life is often likened to a journey. 인생은 종종 여행에 비유된다.

likened a. 비교된, 닮은 syn. compared, similar, identical

Plus Data
likewise ad. 똑같이, 마찬가지로 syn. similarly

Review

☐ flaw

☐ vulnerable

☐ persist

☐ barter

☐ liken

☐ mode

☐ derive

☐ encompass

☐ ultimately

☐ novel

☐ pledge

☐ subside

☐ staple

☐ prestige

☐ impair

☐ shift

☐ outstanding

☐ ooze

☐ tailor

☐ rare

☐ vex

☐ stem from

☐ random

☐ hence

☐ sequent

☐ promising

☐ hollow

☐ pore

☐ simultaneous

☐ hearten

181-210

181 **keen**
[kiːn]

a. 강렬한, 예민한, 예리한, 매우 열중하는
extreme or very strong; very good or well developed; very sharp; eager

[syn] **intense** 강렬한, 예민한 **sharp** 날카로운, 예리한

Dogs have a very **keen** sense of smell.
개는 매우 예민한 후각을 갖고 있다.

keenly ad. 날카롭게 syn. acutely

182 **enhance**
[inhǽns]

v. [가치 · 가격 등을] 올리다
improve the quality, amount, or strength of something

[syn] **improve** 개선하다 **exalt** [가치 · 지위 등을] 높이다 **increase, augment** 증가하다

The measures taken should considerably enhance the residents quality of life.
시행된 조치들은 거주자의 삶의 질을 상당히 개선시켜야만 한다.

183 **discrete**
[diskríːt]

a. 별개의
having a clear independent shape or form

[syn] **separate, distinct** 별개의

The organisms can be divided into discrete categories.
그 유기체들은 별개의 종류로 나누어질 수 있다.

Plus Data
discreet a. 신중한 syn. careful, cautious, judicious, prudent

184 **certain**
[sə́ːrtn]

a. ① 확실한
having no doubt; known to be true; destined or inevitable
② 일정한
particular but not named or described

[syn] **inevitable, assured, specific** 확실한(필연적인, 확신하는, 확정된) **specific but unspecified** 어떤

I'm not absolutely certain, but I think I'm right.
나는 완전히 확신하지 못하지만 옳다고 생각한다.

A certain person has been asking questions about the author. 어떤 사람이 그 작가에 대해 계속 질문을 해오고 있다.

certainly ad. 확실히　syn. surely

185 **expertise**
[èkspərtíːz]

n. 전문 기술, 지식
high level of knowledge or skill

syn special skill, ability 전문 기술, 능력

The company is eager to develop its own expertise in the area of computer programming.
회사는 컴퓨터 프로그래밍 분야에서 자사만의 전문 기술을 발전시키기를 열망한다.

186 **fuse**
[fjuːz]

v. 융합시키다[하다], 녹이다, 녹다
mix together different elements, melt at a high temperature

syn join, combine 결합시키다

Opera and pantomime fuse to create pure magic.
오페라와 판토마임이 순수 마술을 창조하기 위해 결합한다.

fusion n. 혼합　syn. union

Word Root	▸ fus = pour
effusion	n. [사상, 감정 등의] 용솟음, 토로
confuse	v. 혼란시키다
diffuse	v. [빛 따위를] 발산하다
infuse	v. [액체를] 주입하다
refuse	v. 거절하다
profuse	a. 많은, 아낌없는

187 **camouflage**
[kǽməflàːʒ]

n. 위장, 변장
device for concealment or deceit
v. 위장시키다, 숨기다
conceal by the use of disguise or by protective coloring or garments

syn covert [짐승의] 숨는 장소, 덮개　**disguise, mask** 위장 | **hide, conceal** 숨기다

He is an expert in military camouflage.
그는 군사 위장술의 전문가이다.

188 evidence
[évədəns]

n. 증거, 근거
your basis for belief or disbelief
v. 입증하다
prove

[syn] **proof** 증거 **reveal** 드러냄, 게시 | **prove, manifest** 증명하다

Evidence shows that global warming is definitely occurring.
지구온난화 현상이 분명히 일어나고 있다는 것을 보여주는 증거가 있다.

189 typical
[típikəl]

a. 전형적인
showing all the characteristics that you would usually expect from a particular group

[syn] **normal, common, regular, standard, unexceptional, usual, routine, ordinary** 일반적인, 보통의, 예외가 아닌

A **typical** day at the office begins at nine o'clock.
그 사무실의 평소 근무 시간은 9시에 시작된다.

190 exercise
[éksərsàiz]

v. [직무 · 기능 등을] 수행하다, [힘 · 능력 · 권력 등을] 사용하다, 운동하다
carry out or practice, as of jobs and professions; put to a use [one power or influence]; do physical activities to make one body strong and healthy
n. 연습, 운동
physical activities to keep fit; a task performed or problem solved in order to develop skill or understanding

[syn] **practice, use** 실행하다, 사용하다, 행사하다 | **workout** 운동, 힘든 일

For centuries, the Church **exercised** almost unquestioned authority. 수세기 동안 교회는 절대 권위를 행사했다.

191 dispose
[dispóuz]

v. ① 배치하다, ~할 마음이 생기게 하다
place in a particular order; put into a willing or receptive frame mind
② 처분하다
get rid of

[syn] **array, arrange** 배치하다 **incline** ~할 마음이 내키게 하다, 경향이 있다 **discard, eliminate** 버리다, 처분하다

The committee was not **disposed** to hold another meeting.
위원회는 또 다른 회의를 개최하지 않으려 했다.

disposition n. 성질, 경향 syn. temperament, characteristics, preference, tendency, inclination
disposal n. 처분

Word Root	▶ pos = put
compose	v. 구성하다, 쓰다
depose	v. [국왕을] 폐하다, 면직하다
expose	v. 노출시키다
impose	v. [세금 따위를] 부과하다
oppose	v. ~에 반대하다
purpose	n. 목적, 의도
suppose	v. 가정하다, 추측하다

192 **variable**
[vέəriəbl]

a. 변하기 쉬운
liable to or capable of change

syn **unstable, changeable, fickle** 불안정한, 변하기 쉬운, 변덕스러운

Winds will be variable. 바람은 변덕스러울 것이다.

193 **roughly**
[rʌ́fli]

ad. 대략적으로
fairly correct but not exact

syn **approximately, nearly, about, around** 대략적으로, 대략

Roughly half of all working women are mothers.
대략적으로 직업을 가진 여성의 절반은 자녀를 두고 있다.

194 **stationary**
[stéiʃnèri]

a. 움직이지 않는, 정체된
not moving or not changing

syn **fixed, immobile, motionless, stagnant** 고정된, 움직일 수 없는, 움직이지 않는, 정체된

The storm system remained almost stationary just south of the coast. 그 폭풍은 남쪽 해안에 거의 정체해 있었다.

195 **stick to**

v. 고수하다, 달라붙다
keep to; become fixed as if with glue

syn **cling to, adhere to** 달라붙다

The pasta has stuck to the bottom of the pan.
파스타가 팬의 바닥에 눌어붙었다.

sticky a. 끈적끈적한   syn. adhesive, gluey, gummy, pasty, tacky, viscous

196 **surpass**
[sərpǽs]

v. 능가하다, 한도를 넘어서다
do or be better than; go beyond

[syn] **exceed, outrun** 앞서다

India's population now surpasses that of Africa.
인도의 인구는 현재 아프리카의 인구보다 많다.

unsurpassed a. 탁월한, 뛰어난   syn. unrivaled, unequaled, unmatched, superior

197 **in terms of**

[syn] **with respect to, regarding, depending on**
~에 관해서, ~의 점에서는

The savings, both in terms of time and money, could be considerable. 시간과 돈 두 가지 면에서 모두 그 절약 효과는 상당할 것이다.

198 **innovate**
[ínəvèit]

v. 혁신하다, [새로운 사물을] 받아들이다, 시작하다
bring in new ideas or make changes; begin or introduce something new

[syn] **change, transform, invent** 바꾸다, 혁신하다, 창안하다

We must constantly adapt and innovate to ensure success with new ideas. 우리는 새로운 아이디어로 성공하기 위하여 끊임없이 변화에 적응하고 쇄신해야 한다.

innovative a. 혁신적인, 독창적인   syn. original, specialized

199 **notion**
[nóuʃən]

n. 개념, 의지
an idea; a mental image or representation; a belief or opinion

[syn] **concept, idea** 개념 **opinion** 의견

People at that time were not familiar with the notion that women could be equal to men in dealing business matters.
그 시대의 사람들은 업무 관계에서 여성이 남성과 동등하다는 개념에 익숙하지 않았다.

200 **noxious**
[nákʃəs]

a. 유해한, 불건전한
harmful to physical or mental health

[syn] **harmful, poisonous** 유해한 **poignant** 마음에 사무치는
vicious 부도덕한, 옳지 않은

There are many noxious chemical wastes in the river.
강에는 많은 유해한 화학 폐기물들이 있다.

Plus Data
innocuous(↔ noxious) a. 무해한 syn. harmless

---

201 enormous
[inɔ́:rməs]

a. 거대한, 엄청난
extraordinarily large in size, extent, amount, power, or degree

syn **huge, immense, tremendous, vast, great**
거대한, 막대한, 엄청난

Titanic was enormous in her size. 타이타닉호의 규모는 거대했다.

202 fervent
[fɔ́:rvənt]

a. 열렬한
having or showing great emotion or zeal; extremely hot

syn **passionate, ardent, enthusiastic, eager, avid, energetic** 열렬한, 열정적인

I have always been one of his most fervent proponents.
나는 항상 그의 열렬한 지지자 중의 한 사람이었다.

203 hamper
[hǽmpər]

v. 방해하다
prevent the progress or free movement of

syn **prevent, hinder, impede, obstacle, hurdle, interrupt, disrupt, interfere** 방해하다

The search was hampered by heavy snowfall.
조사는 폭설로 방해받았다.

204 estimate
[éstəmèit]

v. 평가하다
form an opinion about; to guess the cost, size, value, etc. of something

syn **calculate roughly, judge, predict, evaluate, appreciate** 평가하다

The dealer estimated the worth of the used car at the low price. 판매상은 중고차에 헐값을 매겼다.

205 critical
[krítikəl]

a. ① 결정적인, 중요한
forming a turning point or having the great importance
② 비판적인
inclined to judge severely and find fault

③ 비평의
giving opinions or judgments
④ 심각한
serious or dangerous

syn **essential, important** 본질적인, 중요한 **unfavorable** 비판적인 **serious** 심각한

Classroom practice is a critical factor in children's learning. 교실 수업은 아이들의 학습에서 중요한 요소이다.

critically ad. 결정적으로 syn. crucially

---

206 **dimension**
[diménʃən]

n. 치수, 국면
any measurable extent; aspect

syn **aspect, measurement, extent, scope** 국면[양상], 치수, 영역, 범위

Doing volunteer work has added a whole new dimension to my life. 자원봉사 활동은 내 인생에 전혀 새로운 면을 더해 주었다.

---

207 **disrupt**
[disrʌ́pt]

v. [사회 등을] 혼란시키다, [통신 · 모임을] 중단시키다
throw into disorder; interfere in someone else's activity

syn **upset, interrupt, disorder** 뒤엎다, 가로막다, 혼란시키다

Protesters tried to disrupt the meeting.
항의자들은 회의를 방해하려고 시도했다.

disrupted a. 훼방당한 syn. interfered with
disruption n. 붕괴, 중단, 혼란

Word Root	▶ rupt = break
abrupt	a. 갑작스러운
bankrupt	a. 파산한 [bank=bench]
corrupt	v. 부패시키다 [cor⟨con=together⟩]
erupt	v. [화산 등이] 폭발하다
interrupt	v. 중단시키다 [inter=between]
rupture	n. 파멸, 불화

---

208 **domestic**
[dəméstik]

a. 가정의, 국내의
belonging or relating to the home; concerning the internal affairs of a nation

syn **home, internal, tamed** 가정의, 국내의, 길든

They set the strict rule to use English as their domestic

language. 그들은 영어를 자국어로 사용하는 엄격한 법칙을 제정했다.

> **Plus Data**
>
> **undomesticated** a. 야생의, 길들이지 않은 syn. undomestic, untamed, uncultivated, wild

209 **specific**
[spisífik]

a. 특정한, 구체적인
particular; stated clearly or in detail

syn **definite, specified, clearly stated, concrete, exact, precise, certain, special, distinctive** 구체적인, 명시된

Spectators are only allowed into specific areas of the stadium. 관중은 경기장의 지정석에만 입장할 수 있다.

> **Plus Data**
>
> specific areas는 지정석이라는 뜻이다. specific은 general(애매한, 막연한)의 반대 개념으로 '구체적'이라는 뜻이며 restricted, limited, pinned-down과 동의어 이다.

210 **flight**
[flait]

n. 비행, 항공여행
an instance of traveling by air; a scheduled trip by plane between designated airports

syn **plane trip** 비행 **escape** 도망

The refugees made a desperate flight to freedom.
망명자들은 자유를 향해 필사적으로 탈출했다.

Review

□ in terms of

□ innovate

□ keen

□ estimate

□ surpass

□ variable

□ fervent

□ hamper

□ fuse

□ critical

□ typical

□ dispose

□ dimension

□ certain

□ flight

□ expertise

□ notion

□ disrupt

□ discrete

□ enhance

□ noxious

□ evidence

□ domestic

□ exercise

□ camouflage

□ roughly

□ stationary

□ specific

□ enormous

□ stick to

211-240

211 dim
[dim]

a. 어둑한, 희미한
lacking in light or clarity

syn faint, weak, ambiguous, uncertain 희미한, 모호한, 불확실한

With the light turned off, the room was very dim.
불이 꺼진 채, 그 방은 아주 어두웠다.

212 enclose
[enklóuz]

v. 둘러싸다
surround completely

syn encompass, surround, include 둘러싸다, 포함하다

The swimming pool was enclosed by a high fence.
풀장은 아주 높은 담장으로 둘러싸여 있었다.

213 harness
[háːrnis]

v. 마구를 채우다, [자연력을] 동력화하다[이용하다]
put a harness on a horse; use the power of

syn utilize, control 이용하다, 제어하다

Although we are harnessing the force of electricity, we still know very little about its effects on us. 비록 우리는 전력을 이용하고 있지만, 그것이 우리에게 미치는 영향에 대해서는 아직도 잘 알지 못한다.

214 earnest
[ə́ːrnist]

a. 진지한
serious or determined; characterized by a firm and humorless belief in one own

syn enthusiastic, heartfelt, sincere, serious, thoughtful 열렬한, 진심의, 진지한, 사려 깊은

When I said I wanted to help you, I was in earnest.
내가 너를 돕고 싶다고 말했을 때 나는 진지했다.

215 obsolete
[àbsəlíːt]

a. 구식의, 쓸모없게 된
no longer in use

syn old-fashioned, out of fashion, antiquated,

unused 구식의, 낡은, 쓸모없는

Most computer hardware rapidly becomes obsolete.
대부분의 컴퓨터 하드웨어는 빨리 구식이 된다.

216 proliferate
[prəlífərèit]

v. 급격히 증가하다
grow or reproduce rapidly

syn **increase, multiply, generate** 증식하다

Fears that nuclear weapons might proliferate bring super power countries into international conference. 핵무기가 증폭될지도 모른다는 두려움에 강대국들은 국제 회의를 열게 될지도 모른다.

proliferation n. 증식, 확산 syn. multiplication

217 redundant
[ridʌ́ndənt]

a. 여분의, 남아도는
more than is needed, desired, or required

syn **superfluous, surplus, unnecessary** 과다한, 여분의, 불필요한

Computers have made our paper records redundant.
컴퓨터는 문서 기록을 불필요하게 만들었다.

Word Root	▶ und, ound = wave
abound	v. 풍부하다, 가득 채우다
inundate	v. 범람시키다
undulate	v. [파도처럼] 움직이다
surround	v. 에워싸다, 둘러싸다

218 refine
[rifáin]

v. 불순물을 없애다
make something pure or improve

syn **improve, purify, process** 개선하다, 정제하다

When the student was blamed for bad speaking style from her teacher, at once she refined her speaking style. 그 학생은 담임 선생님으로부터 안 좋은 말버릇 때문에 혼이 나자마자 말버릇을 고쳤다.

219 rival
[ràivəl]

n. 경쟁자, 필적하는 사람[것] v. 경쟁하다, 필적하다
be in competition with; be as good, clever, etc. as someone or something else

syn **competitor, contender** 경쟁자 | **match, be equal** 비슷하다

The Dallas Cowboys beat their rivals 20-0.
댈러스 카우보이즈가 그들의 경쟁 상대를 20 대 0으로 이겼다.

unrivaled a. 비길 데 없는, 뛰어난 syn. unequaled, unmatched, superior

220 **spur**
[spəːr]

v. 박차를 가하다, 격려하다
cause to do; give heart or courage to do

syn **stimulate, drive, impel, urge, encourage** 자극하다, 추진시키다, 용기를 주다

A business tax cut is needed to spur industrial investment.
사업 세금의 삭감은 산업 투자를 촉진시키기 위해 필요하다.

221 **suspend**
[səspénd]

v. 중지시키다, 매달다
make inoperative or stop; hang

syn **hang** 매달다 **postpone, delay** 미루다 **cease, discontinue, halt** 중지하다 **fear** 누렵게 하다

His license was suspended after a drunk-driving conviction.
그는 음주 운전으로 면허가 정지되었다

suspension n. 미룸, 연기

Plus Data
suspense n. 공포

Word Root ▶ vict, vinc = conquer

convict	v. 유죄로 선고하다 [con=intensive] n. 기결수
convince	v. 확신하게 하다
evict	v. [토지에서 세든 사람을] 쫓아내다 [e=out]
evince	v. [감정 따위를] 나타내다
invincible	a. 정복할 수 없는 [in=not]
vanquish	v. 정복하다 [vanq⟨vanc⟨vinc]
victim	n. 희생자
victory	n. 승리자, 정복자

222 **synthesis**
[sínθəsis]

n. 합성
the combining of separate elements(ideas) or substances to make a whole which is different or new

syn **mixture, union, amalgamation, unit** 혼합, 결합, 융합, 단일체

Their art was a synthesis of Celtic and Mediterranean

traditions. 그들의 예술은 켈트와 지중해 전통이 융합되어 있었다.

223 **wary**
[wέəri]

a. 조심하는
on guard, watchful

syn **cautious, careful, alert** 주의하는, 조심하는, 경계하는

He was wary of putting too much trust in her.
그는 그녀를 너무 많이 신뢰하는 것을 조심했다.

224 **while**
[hwail]

conj. ~하는 동안에, 동시에, 반면에
during the time or at that same time as; despite the fact

syn **whereas, although, even though** 반면에, 비록 ~이지만

The temporary employees for the project didn't display work efficiency while the regular staff members successfully completed their tasks. 정규 직원들은 맡은 일을 완수한 반면에 일용 직원들은 일의 효율성을 보여주지 못했다.

225 **scrupulous**
[skrú:pjuləs]

a. 양심적인, 철저한, 신조가 있는
conscientious and exact; arising from a sense of right and wrong; principled

syn **prudent, careful, cautious, honest** 신중한, 조심성 있는, 양심적인

You must be scrupulous about hygiene when you are preparing a baby's food.
아기의 음식을 준비할 때는 위생에 주의해야 한다.

226 **render**
[réndər]

v. 주다, ~이 되게 하다
give or make available; cause to become

syn **provide, represent, make** 주다, 나타내다

We are sincerely grateful to everyone who has rendered assistance to the victims of the earthquake.
지진 희생자들에게 도움을 준 모두에게 우리는 깊이 감사한다.

227 **realm**
[relm]

n. 영역, 영토
an area of interest or activity; the domain ruled by a king or queen

syn **area, territory, domain, field** 영역

This is not really within the realms of my experience.
이것은 정말로 내 경험의 영역 안에 있지 않다.

228 **indigenous**
[indídʒənəs]

a. 토착의, 타고난
originating where it is found

syn **native, innate, inborn, inherent** 토착의, 타고난

The kangaroo is indigenous to Australia. 캥거루는 호주 토종이다.

Word Root	▶ gen = birth, creation, race, kind
congenial	a. 같은 성질의, 마음 맞는
congenital	a. [병 따위가] 선천적인
degenerate	v. 타락[퇴보]하다
engender	v. 발생시키다, 야기하다
homogeneous	a. 동종의 [homo, iso=same]
ingenious	a. [사람이] 영리한
genial	a. [날씨 등이] 성장에 맞는, 온화한, 따뜻한, 친절한, 다정한
generate	v. 낳다, 산출하다, 야기하다
genius	n. 천재, [타고난] 자질, 경향, 특징
general	a. 일반적인
genuine	a. 진짜의
genetic	a. 유전학의

229 **discard**
[diskά:rd]

v. 없애다
throw away something useless or undesirable

syn **get rid of, throw away, cast off** 없애다, 던져버리다

Remove the seeds from the melon and discard them.
멜론에서 씨를 빼서 버려라.

230 **encroach**
[enkróutʃ]

v. 잠식하다, 침입하다
take another's possessions or rights gradually or stealthily;
advance beyond proper or former limits

syn **invade, intrude, infringe, penetrate, permeate, infiltrate** 잠식하다, 침입하다, 침투하다

Housing developments continue to encroach on wildlife habitats. 주택 개발로 인해 동물의 서식지에 대한 침해가 계속되고 있다.

encroachment n. 침식, 침입 syn. erosion, invasion

Wednesday

231 innocuous
[inάkjuəs]

a. 무해한, 악의 없는
not injurious to physical or mental health; lacking intent

[syn] **harmless** 무해한 **dull, insipid, monotonous** 무미
건조한, 단조로운

Although he was angry with them, his words were an
innocuous remark.
비록 그가 그들에게 화는 냈지만 그의 말이 해가 되지는 않았다.

232 environment
[invάiərənmənt]

n. 환경
the area in which something exists or lives

[syn] **ecology** 생태 **setting, surroundings** 환경 **habitat**
서식지

We need to create a safe working environment for all of
our employees.
우리의 모든 직원에게 안전한 작업 환경을 조성해 줄 필요가 있다.

233 protrude
[proutrú:d]

v. 내밀다
stick out from or through something; extend out; project in
space

[syn] **extend, extrude, jut** 뻗치다,밀어내다[돌출하다], 돌출시키다

She hung her coat on a nail protruding from the wall.
그녀는 코트를 벽에 있는 못에 걸었다.

protruding a. 돌출한 syn. projecting

Word Root	▸ trud, trus = thrust
abstruse	a. 난해한 [abs⟨ab=away⟩]
extrude	v. [사람, 물건을] 밀어내다
intrude	v. 강요하다, 침입하다

234 rather than

[syn] **instead of** 대신에

I think I'll have a cold drink rather than coffee.
나는 커피 대신에 시원한 음료수를 마실 생각이다.

235 unsurpassed
[ʌnsərpǽst]

[syn] **superior, well-trained, unrivaled, unparalleled**
뛰어난, 잘 훈련된, 필적할 수 없는

Twenty miles north there will be a coastline unsurpassed
in its beauty. 20마일 북쪽으로 경관이 아주 빼어난 해안선이 나올 것이다.

236 submarine
[sʌ́blmərìːn]

a. 해저의, 잠수함의 n. 잠수함

syn underwater 수중의 | a ship that can travel under water 잠수함

To put the submarine telephone cable under sea, government spent much money.
해저 전화선을 놓기 위해서 정부는 많은 돈을 썼다.

Plus Data
submerge v. 물에 잠그다 syn. dip, sink

237 retard
[ritάːrd]

v. 늦추다
[cause to] move more slowly or operate at a slower rate

syn delay, slow down, hamper 지연시키다, 중단시키다

Lack of protein may retard children's growth.
단백질의 부족은 어린아이의 성장을 지연시킬 수 있다.

238 procure
[proukjúər]

v. 입수하다
obtain esp. after an effort

syn obtain, acquire, gain, capture, grasp, seize
획득하다

She asked him to procure visas for her family.
그녀는 그에게 그녀 가족을 위해서 비자를 얻을 것을 요청했다.

procurement n. 획득 syn. obtaining

239 network
[nétwə̀ːrk]

n. 조직
an interconnected system of things or people

syn set of connection, system 조직망, 체계

Gold rush caused a network of railroads to develop in the West. 골드러시는 서부에 철도망이 발달하게 만들었다.

240 forage
[fɔ́ːridʒ]

v. 식량을 구하다, 찾아 돌아다니다
go from place to place searching, especially for food
n. 사료, 마초, 먹을 것 찾기
food grown for horses and farm animals

syn search for food, rummage 식량을 찾다, 식량을 찾아 닥치는 대로 뒤지다 | food for horses or cattle 말이나 소의 먹이

They spent their days foraging for food around the city.

그들은 그 도시를 돌아다니며 음식을 찾으러 다니는 데 하루를 다 보냈다.

Review

☐ indigenous

☐ render

☐ enclose

☐ discard

☐ submarine

☐ network

☐ earnest

☐ rather than

☐ encroach

☐ forage

☐ protrude

☐ retard

☐ unsurpassed

☐ procure

☐ innocuous

☐ realm

☐ harness

☐ redundant

☐ dim

☐ environment

☐ wary

☐ rival

☐ refine

☐ obsolete

☐ synthesis

☐ suspend

☐ proliferate

☐ while

☐ scrupulous

☐ spur

241-270

241 lash
[læʃ]

v. ① (끈·밧줄로) 묶다
tie together tightly and firmly
② 후려치다
beat severely with a whip

syn **fasten, tie** 묶다 **whip, beat, pound** 때리다

After lashing the boat to the dock, the sailors ran for shelter from the storm.
부두에 배를 묶은 후 선원들은 폭풍을 피해 피난처로 달렸다.

242 motif
[moutíːf]

n. 주제, 동기, 모티프
a pattern or design; an idea that is used many times in a piece of writing or music

syn **theme, concept, topic** 주제, 동기 **design, pattern, figure** 문양, 모양

They made special and bold patterns based upon cultural themes and motifs.
그들은 문화적인 주제와 동기들에 기초해 특별하고 대담한 양식을 만들었다.

243 recast
[riːkǽst]

v. 고쳐 만들다, 배우를 바꾸다
change the form of something or change an actor in a play or film

syn **transform, change** 변형시키다

The agency has been trying to recast itself in a modern image. 그 중개사는 현대적 이미지로 바꾸려고 노력중이다.

244 parcel out
[páːrsəl]

v. 나누다, 분배하다
divide and give as in small portions

syn **share, distribute, allocate, dispense** 나누다

The father appropriately parceled out the land to his three children. 아버지는 세 자녀에게 토지를 알맞게 나눠주었다.

245 absorb
[əbsɔ́:rb]

v. 흡수하다

take something in gradually; understand facts or ideas completely

[syn] **take in** 흡수하다 **suck, soak, saturate** 빨아들이다, 포화시키다

The timber expands as it absorbs moisture from the atmosphere. 목재는 대기에서 수분을 흡수하면서 팽창한다.

246 advent
[ǽdvent]

n. (중요한 인물·사건 등의) 출현, 도래

the arrival that has been awaited

[syn] **arrival** 도착 **appearance** 등장 **introduction, beginning** 시작

Before the advent of computers, not many people knew how to type.
컴퓨터가 출현하기 전에는 많은 사람들이 어떻게 타이핑하는지 몰랐다.

Word Root	▶ vent, ven = come
circumvent	v. 계획을 방해하다, 법, 규칙, 어려움 따위를 회피하다 [circum=around]
convene	v. [모임 따위를] 소집하다
invent	v. 발명하다, 고안하다
intervene	v. 간섭하다, 조정[중재]하다
prevent	v. 막다[방해]하다

247 blend
[blend]

v. 혼합하다

mix together different elements

[syn] **combine** 결합시키다 **mix** 섞다

Their music blends traditional and modern styles.
그들의 음악은 전통 양식과 현대 양식을 결합시키고 있다.

Plus Data

blend a. 온화한 syn. mild, gentle, modest, moderate

248 breakthrough
[bréikθrù:]

n. 돌파, 타개[책]

making an important discovery or event to improve a situation

[syn] **findings, important discovery, invention** 돌파구 **advance** 진척

Detectives are still waiting for a breakthrough in their

investigations. 탐정들은 아직도 수사의 돌파구를 기다리고 있다.

249 brightness
[bràitnis]

n. 빛남, 밝음
the quality of emitting or reflecting light

syn **radiance** 광채

The distance of Mars from Earth, and hence its brightness vary considerably.
화성과 지구의 거리 그리고 그에 따른 화성의 밝기는 변화가 크다.

Plus Data
brilliance 광명 syn. radiance, splendor

250 chance
[tʃǽns]

n. 기회
a possibility due to a favorable combination of circumstances

syn **likelihood, possibility, probability** 있음직한 가능성

Chances are good that you will win. 당신이 이길 가능성이 아주 많다.

251 conceal
[kənsíːl]

v. 감추다
hold back; prevent from being seen or discovered

syn **hide, cover, mask, obscure** 감추다, 숨기다, 가리다, 어둡게 하다

A long velvet curtain concealed a small doorway.
긴 벨벳 커튼에 작은 문이 가려 있었다.

252 crude
[kruːd]

a. 천연 그대로의, 정제하지 않은
simple not expertly made; not refined or processed
n. 원료, 원유

syn **raw, rough, simple, unrefined** 날것의, 가공치 않은, 조악한 | **raw materials** 원료

Investigators are exploring incorporating materials into procedures used to increase the amount of crude extracted from oil wells. 조사관들은 유정으로부터 뽑아낸 원유의 양을 부풀리기 위해 사용된, 공정에 섞어 넣은 물질을 조사하고 있다.

253 customary
[kʌ́stəmèri]

a. 전통적인, 통례의, 평소의
in accordance with custom; commonly used or practiced;

usual

[syn] **traditional, normal, usual, typical, habitual**

관습에 따른, 보통의, 습관적인

The secretary arranged everything with her customary efficiency. 비서는 그녀의 평소 실력대로 모든 것을 정리했다.

254 **deceptive**
[diséptiv]

a. 속이는, 현혹시키는
making one believe what is not true

[syn] **fraudulent, false, untrue, illusive, misleading, dishonest, deceitful** 사기의, 가짜의, 거짓의, 오도하는, 기만하는

Congressmen passed the new laws against misleading or deceptive advertising.

의회는 오도하거나 속이는 광고를 막는 새로운 법을 통과시켰다.

255 **deem**
[di:m]

v. ~으로 간주하다, ~의 의견을 갖다
keep in mind or convey as a conviction or view

[syn] **consider, think of, believe, judge** ~으로 간주하다

These buildings are deemed to be of architectural importance and must be protected.

이 건물들은 건축적인 면에서 중요성을 지닌 것으로 여겨지므로 보호되어야 한다.

256 **devoid**
[divóid]

a. 전혀 없는
completely lacking; being without something that is necessary or usual

[syn] **empty, deficient, lacking, wanting, without**

비어 있는, 부족한

Rob's face was devoid of any warmth.
롭의 얼굴에는 어떠한 온정도 없었다.

257 **devote**
[divóut]

v. [노력·시간·돈 등을] 바치다, 쏟다
give or apply entirely to something

[syn] **dedicate, apply oneself to** 헌신하다, 몰두하다

He devoted most of his time to his painting.
그는 대부분의 시간을 그림에 몰두했다.

258 diminish
[dimíniʃ]

v. 줄이다, 줄다
reduce or be reduced in size or importance

syn **decrease, reduce, lessen, dwindle, curtail, shrink, contract** 감소하다, 줄어들다

The intensity of the sound diminished gradually.
소리의 강도는 점점 줄어들었다.

259 distinguish
[distíŋgwiʃ]

v. 구별하다, 구별짓다
notice or understand the difference between two things; make different something or someone from another

syn **differentiate** 구별짓다 **detect, discern, notice** 감지하다, 식별하다 **discriminate** 차별하다

The students learn to distinguish a great variety of birds, animals, and plants through the course. 학생들은 그 과목을 이수하면서 매우 다양한 새, 동물 그리고 식물을 구분할 수 있게 된다.

distinguished a. 유명한 syn. famous, eminent, noted, outstanding, exalted, conspicuous

260 distract
[distrǽkt]

v. 주의를 다른 곳으로 돌리다, 괴롭히다
draw one attention away from something; make uneasy or disturbed

syn **divert** 주의를 돌리다 **disturb, trouble, worry, bewilder, perplex** [마음·일 등을] 방해하다, 어지럽히다, 당황하게 하다

The experiment failed because the subjects were exposed to various factors to distract their attention.
그 실험은 그 주제들이 그들 주의를 혼란하게 하는 다양한 요소들에 노출되었기 때문에 실패했다.

Word Root	▸ tract = draw
attract	v. 매혹하다
contract	v. 수축시키다, 축소하다 n. 계약
detract	v. 명성을 떨어뜨리다
extract	v. [노력, 힘으로] 뽑아내다
protract	v. 연장하다
retract	v. 철회하다
subtract	v. [수, 양을] 빼다 [sub=under]
tractable	a. 다루기 쉬운, 유순한

261 **dominate**
[dámənèit]

v. 지배하다
have control over; be the most important

syn **prevail, be prevalent in** 널리 퍼지다 **control, dominer, govern, rule** 압도하다, 지배하다

International drug companies will take a drug policy for the purpose of dominating the tranquilizer market shares.
세계의 제약 회사들은 진정제 시장을 점유하기 위한 제약 정책들을 마련할 것이다.

dominated a. 지배적인, 압도적인 syn. prevalent, overwhelming, prevailing

262 **dwindle**
[dwíndl]

v. 감소하다, [가치 등이] 없어지다
become smaller or lose substance

syn **decrease, diminish, abate, lessen, shorten**
감소하다, 줄어들다

Membership of the club has dwindled from 70 to 20.
그 클럽 회원 수는 70명에서 20명으로 감소했다.

dwindled a. 감소된 syn. decreased

263 **engage**
[ingéidʒ]

v. [남을] ~에 종사[관여]시키다, 관여하다, 약속하다
employ or involve someone; involve oneself, be involved in; devote attention and effort, pledge or promise, esp, to marry

syn **hire, involve, apply (oneself)** 고용하다, 관여시키다[하다], 몰두하다

The company is to engage a new sales director.
그 회사는 새로운 판매 책임자를 고용할 것이다.

Plus Data
dismiss(↔ engage) v. 해고하다, 면직하다 syn. fire, lay off, discharge, unseat

264 **enthusiasm**
[enθú:ziæzm]

n. 열정
great excitement for or interest in a subject

syn **intense interest, passion, fervor, zeal** 열정

Clark Moor's enthusiasm for music has stayed strong throughout his 23 years in radio. 클라크 무어의 음악에 대한 열정은 라디오에 몸담고 있는 23년 내내 식을 줄 모르고 있다.

enthusiastic a. 열정적인　syn. eager, passionate, avid, energetic, ardent

265 **erect**
[irékt]

v. 건설하다, 똑바로 세우다
construct; cause to rise up

syn **raise, build, construct** 세우다

A memorial to Mother Teresa was erected after her death.
마더 테레사 수녀의 기념비는 그녀의 사후에 세워졌다.

erected a. 똑바로 세운

Plus Data
elect　v. 뽑다, 선출하다　syn. select, choose, vote

266 **fashion**
[fǽʃən]

n. 유행, 방식
the latest style in clothes, cosmetics, hairs, and etc.; a manner of performance
v. 형성하다, 맞추다
give shape or form to; adapt to a purpose or an occasion

syn **shape** 형태 **mode, style, trend, fad** 유행 | **shape, make, create** 만들다 **be the rage** 유행이다

The ballerina moves in a graceful fashion.
발레리나는 우아하게 움직이고 있다.

fashionable a. 유행하는　syn. popular

267 **fertile**
[fə́ːrtl]

a. 비옥한, [생물이] 번식력이 있는, 다산의
capable of reproducing; bearing in abundance, esp. offspring

syn **rich** 풍부한 **productive, prolific, fruitful** 결실이 많은

This is surely fertile ground for experimentation.
이곳은 실험하기에 적합한 매우 비옥한 토양이다.

fertility n. 비옥, 풍요
fertilizer n. 비료

Plus Data
barren(↔ fertile)　a. 토양이 척박한, 수정이 되지 않는　syn. sterile

268 **fortified**
[fɔ́ːrtəfàid]

syn **strengthened** 강화된

The police resumed the search, fortified by a hearty breakfast. 경찰은 아침식사를 양껏 먹고 나서 원기를 회복하여 조사를 재개했다.

fortify v. 강화하다 syn. strengthen, consolidate

fort n. 성벽, 요새

269 **imaginable**
[imǽdʒənəbl]

a. 상상이 가는
possible to imagine

syn **conceivable** 생각할 수 있는

Adults did not admit a situation that was hardly imaginable ten years ago.
어른들은 10년 전에는 상상하기도 힘든 그 상황을 받아들이지 않았다.

imaginative a. 상상력이 풍부한 syn. creative

270 **importance**
[impɔ́ːrtəns]

n. 중요성
the quality of being important

syn **significance, consequence** 중요성

By 1800s, the monarchy had declined in importance.
1800년대에 이르렀을 때 왕권은 이미 쇠퇴해 있었다.

important a. 중요한, 근본적인 syn. significant, consequential, major, meaningful, influential, notable, critical, serious, vital, principal

Review

☐ diminish

☐ devoid

☐ imaginable

☐ dwindle

☐ distract

☐ enthusiasm

☐ absorb

☐ importance

☐ dominate

☐ breakthrough

☐ fashion

☐ erect

☐ fortified

☐ engage

☐ fertile

☐ motif

☐ recast

☐ lash

☐ parcel out

☐ chance

☐ brightness

☐ blend

☐ customary

☐ crude

☐ deceptive

☐ advent

☐ deem

☐ distinguish

☐ devote

☐ conceal

271-300

---

271 inaccessible
[ìnəksésəbl]

a. 접근하기 어려운
capable of being reached only with great difficulty or not at all

syn **unreachable, unattainable** 도달하기 어려운 **difficult to understand** 이해하기 어려운

Much of Shakespeare's language is inaccessible for today's students.
셰익스피어의 언어는 상당 부분이 오늘날의 학생들에게 이해하기 어렵다.

---

272 dangle
[dǽŋgl]

v. 매달려 늘어지다, 매달아 늘어뜨리다
hang loosely; hold something so that it hangs loosely

syn **hang** 매달다 **lash, tie** 바짝 묶다

A single light bulb dangled from the ceiling.
한 개의 백열전구가 천장에 늘어져 있었다.

---

273 habitat
[hǽbitæ̀t]

n. 서식지, 거주지
the type of environment an organism or group lives or occurs

syn **home, dwelling, lodging, quarters, residence** 거주지 **place, locality, territory, environment** 장소, 소재지, 영토, 환경

There is a rare bird in danger of losing its natural habitat.
자연 서식지를 잃어버릴 위험에 처해 있는 희귀종 새가 있다.

habitation n. 거주 syn. dwelling
habitant n. 거주자 syn. resident, dweller, tenant

---

274 ideal
[aidíːəl]

a. 이상적인
without fault or the best possible

syn **perfect, suitable, fitting, model, exemplary** 이상적인, 완전한, 모범적인

The job fair provides an ideal opportunity for jobseekers and employers to meet.
취업 박람회는 구직자와 고용주가 만날 수 있는 아주 좋은 기회를 제공한다.

---

ideally ad. 완전히 syn. perfectly

275 **erratic**
[irǽtik]

a. 변덕스러운
liable to sudden, unpredictable change

syn **irregular** 불규칙적인 **inconsistent** 앞뒤가 맞지 않는
shifting 이리저리 움직이는

Tom Wilkins is a good player but erratic.
톰 윌킨스는 훌륭한 연주자이지만 성격이 변덕스럽다.

erratically ad. 불규칙적으로 syn. irregularly

276 **haul**
[hɔːl]

v. 끌어당기다
draw slowly or heavily

syn **pull, drag, draw** 끌다 **tow** 견인하다

Rescue workers attached the men to ropes before
hauling them to safety.
구조 요원들은 사람들을 줄에 묶은 뒤 천천히 끌어올려 구조했다.

hauled a. 당겨진 syn. pulled, carried

277 **height**
[hait]

n. 절정
the highest level or degree attainable

syn **peak, pinnacle** 정점 **altitude** 고도

Now the actress is the height of her career.
현재 그 여배우는 배우로서 전성기를 맞고 있다.

278 **drought**
[draut]

n. 가뭄
a long period when there is little or no rain

syn **lack of water** 가뭄

Austin, Texas experienced the severe and long period of
drought last summer.
텍사스 주의 오스틴 시는 지난 여름 혹독하고 긴 가뭄을 겪었다.

279 **impression**
[impréʃən]

n. 인상, 효과, 영향, [막연한] 느낌, 생각, 기억
the way that something seems, looks, or feels; an opinion of
what something is like

syn **image** 인상 **influence, effect, impact** 영향, 효과

feeling 느낌 **notion** 의견

As a serious candidate, you want to make a good
impression on everyone you meet.
당신은 진지한 후보자로서 만나는 모든 사람에게 좋은 인상을 주길 원한다.

impressive adj. 인상적인 syn. striking, characteristic

---

280 **innate**
[inéit]

a. 타고난
present at birth but not necessarily hereditary

syn **inborn** 타고난 **natural** 천성의 **congenital** [병·결함 등이]
선천적인

His innate sense of justice made him popular with his
workforce. 그의 타고난 정의감은 그로 하여금 동료들에게 인기를 끌게 했다.

---

281 **incise**
[insàiz]

v. 절개하다, 새기다
cut the surface of; engrave into a surface

syn **cut into, carve** 새기다

Native Americans made one of the most beautiful things
in the world of pottery, and they incised many designs on
the clay. 인디언들은 도자기 세계에서 가장 아름다운 것들 중의 하나를 만들었다.
그리고 그들은 도자기 위에 여러 가지 도안들을 새겨 넣었다.

Word Root	▶ cis = cut
concise	a. 간결한 [con=intensive, together]
decisive	a. 결정적인, 단호한 [de=down]
excise	v. [몸의 일부를] 잘라내다, [문장 따위를] 삭제하다
precise	a. 정밀한, 꼼꼼한 [pre=before, intensive]

---

282 **intent**
[intént]

n. 의도, 의도된 것
the intended meaning of a communication; an anticipated
outcome that is intended

syn **aim, purpose, intention, attempt, plan** 의도,
의향

She denies possessing the drug with intent to supply.
그녀는 공급할 의도로 약을 소지하고 있다는 것을 부인한다.

283 **intimacy**
[íntəməsi]

n. 친밀, 친교
a feeling of being intimate and belonging together; close or warm friendship

[syn] **close familiarity** 친밀

Their tone suggests there's a deepening intimacy between them. 그들의 목소리에서 서로 깊은 친분이 있다는 것이 나타난다.

intimate a. 친밀한 syn. familiar, friendly, favorable
intimately ad. 친밀하게 syn. closely

284 **institute**
[ínstətʃùːt]

v. 세우다
set up or lay the groundwork for

[syn] **establish** 만들다, 설치하다 **initiate, start** 시작하다
introduce 소개하다

The Democratic Party said it had instituted new security measures for its staff.
민주당은 당원을 위한 새로운 안전 대책을 마련했다고 말했다.

institution n. 제도, 설립 syn. establishment

285 **intrigue**
[intríːg]

v. 흥미를 유발시키다
cause to be interested or curious

[syn] **fascinate, interest, confuse** 매혹하다, 흥미를 일으키다, 혼란시키다

The idea intrigued office members.
그 생각은 사무실 직원들을 술렁이게 했다.

intriguing a. 흥미로운 syn. attractive

Friday

Word Root ▸ tric, trigu = petty obstacle

extricate   v. [위험·곤경으로부터] 구출하다, 해방하다
intricate   a. 뒤얽힌, 복잡한

---

286 **key**
[ki:]

a. 중요한, 본질적인, 기본적인
serving as an essential component

[syn] **important, central** 중요한

Education is likely to be a key issue in the next election.
교육은 아마도 다음 선거에서 중요한 쟁점이 될 것이다.

---

287 **mechanism**
[mékənìzm]

n. 수단, 방법
a way of doing something; technical aspects of doing something

[syn] **device, means** 수단 **process** 과정

When trading partners dispute the problem on the price of the goods, negotiation is a unique mechanism for settling disputes between them. 상품의 가격 문제를 놓고 거래 당사자들 간에 논쟁이 벌어지면, 절충하여 협상하는 길만이 유일한 방법이다.

---

288 **moreover**
[mɔːróuvər]

ad. 게다가, 더욱이
also and more importantly

[syn] **additionally, in addition** 게다가 **furthermore** 더욱이

Bicycling is good exercise. Moreover, it doesn't pollute the air. 자전거 타기는 좋은 운동이다. 게다가 그것은 공기를 오염시키지도 않는다.

---

289 **on occasion**

[syn] **once in a while, periodically** 수시로, 때때로

He continues to work with us on occasion.
그는 계속해서 우리와 때때로 일하고 있다.

---

290 **optimal**
[áptəməl]

a. 최적의
most favorable or desirable

[syn] **advantageous** 유리한, 이로운 **desirable** 바람직한

The patient is advised to do some physical activity three

times a week for optimal health. 그 환자는 최적의 건강을 유지하기 위해 일주일에 3회는 운동을 하도록 권고 받고 있다.

291 ordinary
[ɔ́ːrdənèri]

a. 보통의, 평범한, 여느 때와 같은
not different or special in any way

syn **unexceptional, mundane** 일상의 **normal, usual, common, regular, typical** 일반적인

It was just an ordinary Saturday morning.
그저 일상적인 토요일 아침이었다.

292 origin
[ɔ́ːrədʒin]

n. 시작, 원인
the beginning or cause of something

syn **beginning, root, source** 시작, 기원

Meteorites may hold clues about the origin of life on Earth. 유성에 지구상의 생명체의 기원에 관한 실마리가 들어 있을지 모른다.

originate v. 시작하다 syn. start, begin, initiate, commence, launch, take off

293 out of the question

완전히 불가능한, 물어보나마나한
totally unlikely; impossible; not worth considering

syn **impossible** 불가능한

Taking a holiday is out of the question; you'll have to arrange it for some other time.
휴가를 내는 것은 불가능합니다. 다른 날로 조정해야 할 것입니다.

294 ominous
[ámənəs]

a. 불길한
threatening or suggesting evil or tragic developments

syn **threatening, unpromising** 위협하는, 불길한

Last night, we had much rain and lighting, after then there was an ominous silence.
지난 밤 우리는 많은 비와 번개를 맞았다. 그리고 나서 불길한 정적이 찾아왔다.

omen n. 나쁜 징조

Plus Data

auspicious(↔ ominous) a. 좋은 일이 일어날 것 같은, 길조의
syn. favorable, fortunate, lucky, opportune

295 ignite
[ignàit]

v. 불을 붙이다, 불이 붙다, 자극하다
[cause to] start burning; excite feelings or passions

syn **set on fire** 불을 붙이다 **catch fire** 불이 붙다 **stimulate, stir up** 자극하다

The fire was ignited by a spark from an electrical fault.
화재는 전기 과실로 발생한 불꽃에서 불이 붙었다.

296 incorporate
[inkɔ́ːrpərèit]

v. 합치다, 포함하다
make into a whole; have as a component

syn **combine** 합치다 **include** 포함하다

The course incorporates a strong German language element. 그 과목은 독일어가 상당히 많이 쓰인다.

297 deposit
[dipázit]

v. 예금하다, 두다
put into a bank account; leave something somewhere

syn **lay down, place, put** 놓다, 쌓다 | **saving** 저축

They deposited their luggage at the hotel.
그들은 그 호텔에 여장을 풀었다.

298 override
[òuvəráid]

v. ① 무효로 하다, 무시하다
refuse to accept previous decision, an order, etc.
② ~에 우선하다
prevail over; be greater or more important than

syn **cancel, annul, nullify** 무효로 하다 **overturn, reverse** 뒤집다 **overwhelm** 압도하다 **outweigh** 더 중요하다

Budgetary concerns overrode all other considerations.
예산 문제는 다른 모든 고려할 사항보다 더 중요했다.

299 hectic
[héktik]

a. 열광적인, 몹시 바쁜
full of activity; marked by intense emotion; very busy and fast

syn **feverish** 열띤 **frantic, ardent, fervent, frenzied, passionate** 열렬한 **very busy** 매우 바쁜

The two days we spent there were enjoyable but hectic.
그곳에서 우리가 보낸 이틀은 즐거웠지만 매우 바빴다.

300 **myriad**
[míriəd]

too many to be counted; composed of diverse elements
a vast number of something

syn **many, numerous, innumerable** 무수한 | **variety**
다양함

Myriad treasures are believed to be buried beneath the
sea. 사람들은 수많은 보물들이 그 바다 밑에 묻혀 있다고 믿고 있다.

Review

□ key

□ erratic

□ on occasion

□ moreover

□ origin

□ hectic

□ ideal

□ out of the question

□ ominous

□ mechanism

□ drought

□ incorporate

□ optimal

□ ignite

□ myriad

□ inaccessible

□ innate

□ haul

□ habitat

□ intimacy

□ institute

□ incise

□ impression

□ dangle

□ deposit

□ height

□ ordinary

□ intent

□ intrigue

□ override

Weekend

인문 II 인류학, 고고학, 도시학

Anthropology
인류학

adaptive 적응하는

acquired 후천적인, 학습된

adjustment 조절, 적응(↔ **natural** 선천적인)

ancestor 조상

animism 애니미즘(모든 자연물이나 자연 현상에 정령이 있다고 믿는 것)

biological anthropology 생물학적 인류학

class 계급

cultural anthropology 문화 인류학

descendent 후손

epic 서사시

folk story 민간 설화

hereditary 세습의, 유전의

legend 전설

matrilineal 모계의 **matriarchy** 모계제 (↔ **patriarchy** 부계제)

medieval 중세의

monarchy 군주제

myth 신화

organism 유기적 조직체

phenomena 현상

pluralism 다원론

prehistoric 역사 이전의

primitive people 원시인

status 신분, 지위

tribe 부족, 종족

Archaeology
고고학

aboriginal 원주민의

anachronism 시대 착오

artifact 인공물, 문화 유물

Bronze Age 청동기 시대

charcoal 목탄

chronology 연대기

date 연대를 측정하다

deform 변형시키다

diggings 발굴물

excavate 발굴하다

extinct 멸종한

flourish 번영하다

flowering 번영

hierarchy 계급제도

hieroglyph 상형문자

hominoid 유인원

implement 도구

Mesolithic 중석기 시대의

metallic 금속의

mound 고분

Neolithic 신석기 시대의

origin 기원

Paleolithic 구석기 시대의

philology 문헌학

polyphony 다성 음악

prevalent 널리 퍼져있는

relics 유물

remain 유물

ruins 유적

scraper 긁어내는 도구

site 유적지

skeletal 해골의

specimen 표본

strata 유적층

stratigraphy 지층학

turmoil 소란, 소동

unearth 발굴하다, 파다

Urban Studies

도시학

authorities 당국

autonomy 자치

bureaucracy 관료제

census 인구 조사

charity 자선

civic movement 시민 운동

collective behavior 집단 행동

community 지역사회

concentrate 집중하다

congestion 혼잡, 과잉

consensus 합의

cultural bias 문화적 편견

demography 인구 통계학

evolution 발전, 진전

exodus 집단적 이동

expansive 확장해 가는

explosion 폭발

metropolitan 대도시의

outer city 외곽 도시

pollution 공해

population 인구

prosperity 번영, 융성

region 지역

relocation 이주

resident 거주자

satellite 위성도시

sect 분파

secular 세속의

slump 불황, 폭락

social behavior 사회적 행동

stock 주식 bond 채권

stock exchange 증권 거래소

subjective 주관적인

suburb 교외 *cf.* suburbanization 근교화

surplus 잉여

tariff 관세

transaction 상거래

3rd week

301-330

301 **peripheral**
[pərífərəl]

a. 주변적인, 주변의
related to the key issue but not of central importance; on or near an edge

[syn] **marginal, surrounding** 주변의

The talks made progress on peripheral issues but failed to resolve the main dispute between the two sides.
그 회담은 주변적인 문제들에서는 진전을 보였지만 양측 사이에 놓여 있는 가장 큰 분쟁은 해결하지 못했다.

keenly ad. 날카롭게 syn. acutely

Plus Data
central(↔ peripheral) a. 중심의 syn. main

302 **preserve**
[prizə́:rv]

v. 보존하다
keep in perfect or unaltered condition; cause to remain or last

[syn] **maintain, sustain, conserve** 유지하다, 보존하다

The society works to preserve the district's historic buildings.
그 지방 공동체는 그 지역의 역사적인 건물들을 보존하기 위한 활동을 벌이고 있다.

303 **recruit**
[rikrú:t]

v. 고용하다, 모집하다
seek to employ; register formally as a member

[syn] **employ** 고용하다 **enlist** 모병하다 **draft** 징병하다
muster, gather [병사·선원] 등을 집합시키다, 모으다 **obtain** 얻다

The police are trying to recruit more Afro-American and Asian officers. 경찰은 흑인과 아시아계 경찰관을 모집하고 있는 중이다.

recruiting a. 획득한 syn. obtaining

304 **proper**
[prápər]

a. 알맞은
satisfactory, suitable or correct

syn **suitable, appropriate** 알맞은

You have to have the proper tools for the job.
작업에 알맞은 도구를 사용해야 한다.

properly ad. 알맞게 syn. appropriately, correctly

305 clout
[klaut]

n. 때림, 권력
power and influence over other people or events

v. 때리다, 치다
hit someone or something with the hand or with a heavy object

syn **influence, power** 영향력 | **hit, beat** 때리다

Government has more political clout than the opposition party on this issue.
정부는 이 문제에 대해 야당보다 더 큰 정치적 영향력을 가지고 있다.

306 in operation

syn **being used** 사용되는, 시행중인 **present** 현재의

Many factories in operation ran a risk on the basis of bad economic situation during Great Depression.
대공황 동안에는 조업을 하고 있던 많은 공장들이 경제 사정이 좋지 않았기 때문에 위험 요소를 안고 있었다.

operation n. 작업, 작동, 작용(the fact of working; being active; or having an effect)

307 vigorous
[vígərəs]

a. 정력적인, 원기 왕성한, 활기찬
strong and active physically or mentally

syn **strong, robust, hardy** 강건한, 강력한 **energetic**
활발한, 열정적인

We need a vigorous campaign to reduce deaths on the roads.
교통 사망자 수를 줄이기 위한 활발한 캠페인이 필요하다.

vigorously ad. 열정적으로 syn. energetically

308 agile
[ǽdʒəl]

a. 재빠른, 두뇌가 빠른, 경쾌한
moving quickly and lightly; mentally quick; playful like a lively kitten

syn **quick, rapid, nimble** 재빠른 **active, frisky, briskly**
경쾌한

The ferret is an agile hunter. 흰족제비는 민첩한 사냥꾼이다.

309 **decisive**
[disàisiv]

a. 결정적인, 명확한

determining or having the power to determine an outcome; beyond doubt, unmistakable

syn **crucial, critical, vital, important** 결정적인, 중요한
definite 명확한

The U.S. has played a decisive role in these negotiations.
미국은 이 협상들에서 결정적인 역할을 해 왔다.

Word Root ▶ cis = cut

concise	a. 간결한 [con=intensive, together]
excise	v. [몸의 일부를] 잘라내다, (문장 따위를) 삭제하다
incise	v. 절개하다, 조각하다 [in=in, into]
precise	a. 정밀한, 꼼꼼한 [pre=before, intensive]

310 **commence**
[kəméns]

v. 시작하다

begin; take the first step in carrying out an action

syn **begin, initiate, launch, generate, originate, start** 시작하다

The lawyers are preparing for the trial, which commences in 30 days. 변호사들은 30일 후에 시작하는 그 재판을 준비하는 중이다.

Plus Data

commerce n. 상업, 사업 syn. trade, business
comment v. 언급하다, 비평하다 syn. remark, state
commend v. 칭찬하다 syn. acclaim, applaud, compliment, praise

311 **conscious**
[kánʃəs]

a. 의식하고 있는

having awareness of surroundings, sensations, and thoughts

syn **sensible, discerning, aware** 통찰력이 있는
knowledgeable 지식이 있는 **deliberate, intentional** 고의적인

The actor wasn't consciously trying to upset the audience.
그 배우가 일부러 관중을 실망시키려고 한 것은 아니다.

consciously ad. 의식적으로 syn. intentionally, purposefully

312 capitalize
[kǽpətəlàiz]

v. 자금을 대다, 이용하다
supply with capital; draw advantage from

syn enlarge 확대하다 **take advantage of, exploit, utilize, gain** 자기 이익에 이용하다

He is trying to capitalize on popular discontent with the current administration.
그는 현 정부에 대해 만연해 있는 대중의 불만을 이용하려고 한다.

313 designate
[dézignèit]

v. 가리키다
point out; give a name or title to; select and set aside for a duty, an office, or a purpose

syn indicate, appoint, nominate, name, choose
지명하다, 임명하다

Picnicking is only allowed in designated areas.
피크닉은 지정된 장소에서만 허용됩니다.

designated a. 지정된,할당된 syn. allocated, chosen, nominated
designation n. 지명, 확인 syn. identification

314 entail
[intéil]

v. 수반하다, [노력 · 비용 등을] 들게 하다
have as a logical consequence

syn involve 포함하다 **require** 요구하다, 불가피하다

All mergers entail some job losses.
모든 합병은 얼마간의 실직을 포함한다.

entailed a. 연루된 syn. involved

315 evident
[évədənt]

a. 명백한, 분명한
clearly apparent or obvious to the mind or senses

syn apparent, noticeable, obvious, perceptible, definite 명백한, 분명한

The threat of inflation is already evident in bond prices.
물가 상승의 우려가 벌써부터 주가에 뚜렷이 나타나고 있다.

316 favor
[féivər]

n. 호의, 지지
friendly regard, approval, or support

v. 친절을 베풀다, 호의적이다
perform a kindness; regard or treat with friendship, approval, or support

syn **approval** 승인 **support** 지지, 지원 | **support, prefer**
지지하다, 호의적이다

The French say that they favor a transition to democracy.
프랑스 국민들은 민주주의로의 변화를 찬성한다고 말한다.

Plus Data
in favor of ~에 찬성하는

---

317 **foliage**
[fóuliidʒ]

n. 잎
the leaves of a plant or tree

syn **leaves** 잎 **vegetation** 야채

Never have they seen the beautiful flowers and dark green foliage in their mother country.
그들은 모국에서는 그와 같이 아름다운 꽃과 짙은 녹음을 한번도 본 적이 없었다.

318 **guide**
[gaid]

v. 안내하다, 시도하나
serve as a guide, direct the course of; exert control or influence over, supervise the training or education of

syn **direct, lead, pilot, conduct** 지도하다, 인도하다

Harry tried to guide the discussion toward some form of compromise. 해리는 그 토론이 타협에 이르도록 인도하려고 애썼다.

guided a. 안내인을 동반한, 유도된, 유도 장치가 붙은 syn. directed

319 **incongruous**
[inkáŋgruəs]

a. 어울리지 않는, 모순된, 부조화의
lacking in harmony, compatibility, or appropriateness

syn **inappropriate, unsuitable** 부적당한 **inconsistent**
조화되지 않는 **conflicting, contradictory, incompatible**
상충되는

The boy was small and fragile and looked incongruous in a training suit. 그 소년은 작고 허약해서 훈련복이 어색해 보였다.

320 **leisurely**
[líːʒərli]

a. 느긋한, 여유 있는
not hurried or forced

syn **slow, slow moving, relaxing, unhurried** 느긋한,
여유 있는

I took a long leisurely walk along the beach.
나는 해변을 따라 천천히 오랫동안 산책했다.

321 monitor
[mánətər]

v. 감시[관리]하다, 검토하다
keep an eye on; watch and check a situation carefully for a period of time in order to discover something about it

syn **check, control, govern, supervise** 조절하다, 관리하다, 통제하다

He will monitor and review company policy.
그는 회사의 정책을 감독하고 점검할 것이다.

322 outrage
[àutreidʒ]

v. 분노하게 하다
cause to feel very angry

syn **anger, enrage, incense** 몹시 화나게 하다 **offend** 감정을 상하게 하다 **insult** 모욕하다

There was public outrage over the killings.
시민들은 그 살인 사건에 대해 분개했다.

outrageous adj. 지나친, 난폭한 syn. extraordinary, excessive, immoderate

323 predicament
[pridíkəmənt]

n. 곤경
difficult and unpleasant situation

syn **difficulty, crisis, dilemma, plight** 어려움, 곤란

I understood her predicament, but there was nothing I could do.
나는 그녀의 어려움을 이해했다. 그러나 내가 할 수 있는 것은 아무것도 없었다.

324 reciprocal
[risíprəkəl]

a. 상호간의
concerning each of two or more persons or things

syn **mutual, complementary, shared** 상호간의, 보충의, 공유의

The department said many countries had a reciprocal agreement for health care with U.S. 그 부서는 많은 국가들이 미국과 보건의료 서비스에 대한 상호 협정을 맺고 있다고 밝혔다.

325 reveal
[riví:l]

v. 드러내다
make known or show something that is surprising or that was previously secret

syn **uncover, unveil, expose, disclose, divulge** 드러내다, 발견하다

She refused to reveal the contents of the letter.
그녀는 그 편지의 내용을 밝히기를 거부했다.

326 **repel**
[ripél]

v. 쫓아버리다
cause to move back by force or influence

syn **drive away, keep at bay** 쫓아내다 **deter, resist**
막다

The wheat is genetically engineered to repel insects.
그 밀은 해충을 방어할 수 있도록 유전자 조작이 되어 있다.

repulsion n. 격퇴
repulsive a. 혐오감을 일으키는

Word Root   ▶ pel, peal = drive

compel	v. 억지로 ~시키다
dispel	v. [불길한 생각을] 쫓아버리다, 분산시키다
expel	v. 내쫓다
impel	v. 추진시키다
propel	v. 추진하다
repellent	a. 불쾌한, 반발하는

327 **source**
[sɔ:rs]

n. 근원, 원인
the place where something begins; the cause of something

syn **origin, beginning, foundation, basis** 근원, 시초,
토대, 기초

The best sources of potassium are vegetables and fruit.
칼륨의 가장 좋은 소스는 야채와 과일이다.

328 **support**
[səpɔ́:rt]

v. 지지하다, 후원하다
approve of; give encouragement; provide the money needed

syn **maintain, sustain** 지탱하다 **bolster, brace, prop,**
strengthen 떠받치다 | **prop, backing, encouragement**
후원, 지지

The United Nations has supported efforts to return the
refugees peacefully.
유엔은 피난민들을 평화적으로 돌려보내기 위한 노력들을 지지해 왔다.

329 thrill
[θril]

n. 전율, 설렘
an almost pleasurable sensation of fright

syn **suspense** 공포 **excitement** 흥미

Winning in Sydney gave her the biggest thrill yet.
시드니에서의 승리는 그녀에게 이제껏 가장 큰 전율을 주었다.

330 unbearable
[ʌnbɛ́ərəbl]

a. 참을 수 없는
so unpleasant or painful to bear

syn **insufferable, insupportable, intolerable, unendurable** 참을 수 없는

Sometimes the young generation are likely to get very angry with a few unbearably difficult situations.
젊은 세대는 때때로 견디기 어려운 상황이 몇 가지 겹쳐오면 크게 분노하기 쉽다.

Review

☐ favor

☐ outrage

☐ preserve

☐ incongruous

☐ guide

☐ leisurely

☐ predicament

☐ foliage

☐ monitor

☐ repel

☐ reciprocal

☐ reveal

☐ source

☐ support

☐ unbearable

☐ peripheral

☐ clout

☐ recruit

☐ decisive

☐ vigorous

☐ in operation

☐ evident

☐ commence

☐ agile

☐ designate

☐ conscious

☐ entail

☐ capitalize

☐ proper

☐ thrill

331-360

331 **potential**
[pəténʃəl]

a. 가능한, 잠재력이 있는
existing in possibility; expected to become or be

syn **possible, probable, latent** 가능성 있는, 잠재적인

The disease is a potential killer. 그 병은 잠재적인 살인자이다.

potentially adv. 잠재적으로, 어쩌면 syn. possibly

332 **propose**
[prəpóuz]

v. 제의[제안]하다
present for consideration

syn **make suggestion, suggest, hold** 제안하다

Einstein proposed his theory of general relativity in 1915.
아인슈타인은 1915년에 그의 일반 상대성 이론을 제시했다.

proposition n. 제안 syn. suggestion

333 **renowned**
[rináund]

a. 유명한, 명성 있는
widely known and esteemed

syn **celebrated, noted, distinguished, acknowledged, famous, eminent, prominent** 유명한

The program includes a performance by the world-renowned Berlin Philharmonic Orchestra. 프로그램에는 세계적으로 유명한 베를린 필하모닉 오케스트라의 연주가 포함되어 있다.

334 **significant**
[signífikənt]

a. 중요한
important in effect or meaning

syn **substantial, important, considerable** 중요한

Davis was one of the most significant musicians of the last century.
데이비스는 지난 세기를 살았던 가장 중요한 음악가 중의 한 명이었다.

335 **sturdy**
[stə́:rdi]

a. [신체가] 강건한, [사물 등이] 견고한
physically strong and solid or thick, so unlikely to break or be

hurt; strong and determined

[syn] **strong, powerful, robust** 튼튼한

Although the elephant moves slow, it has four sturdy legs. 비록 코끼리는 천천히 움직이지만, 네 개의 튼튼한 다리를 가지고 있다.

336 **vanish**
[vǽniʃ]

v. 사라지다

get lost, esp. without warning or explanation

[syn] **disappear, fade away, evaporate** 사라지다

One moment she was there, and then she had vanished. 그녀는 잠깐 동안 거기에 있다가 사라져버렸다.

Plus Data
banish v. 추방하다 syn. expel, depart, exile, drive out

337 **aim**
[eim]

v. 목표로 삼다, 시망하나

direct toward an intended goal

[syn] **intend, plan, attempt** 의도하다, 시도하다 | **goal** 목적

The project aims to provide an outlet for children's creativity.
그 프로젝트는 어린이들이 창의성을 표출할 기회를 마련해 주는 것이 목적이다.

aimed a. 의도된 syn. attempted

338 **classify**
[klǽsəfài]

v. 분류하다, 등급을 매기다

place into a category

[syn] **categorize, sort** 분류하다

The books in the library are classified according to subject. 도서관에 있는 책들은 주제별로 분류되어 있다.

classified adj. 분류한, 항목별의 syn. grouped

339 **territorial**
[tèrətɔ́ːriəl]

a. 영토의, 사유지의

of or relating to a territory

[syn] **terrestrial, land, regional** 땅의, 육지의, 지역의

Both Chile and Argentina feel very strongly about their territorial claims to Antarctica.
칠레와 아르헨티나 양국은 남극에 대한 그들의 영토권을 매우 강하게 주장하고 있다.

territory n. 지역, 영토　syn. region, land, terrain

340 backbone
[bǽkbòun]

n. 등뼈, 중추; [사물의] 중요 요소
the spine; the most important part

[syn] **foundation, basis** 근간, 기초　**spine** 등뼈

Ordinary volunteers form the backbone of most charitable organizations.
평범한 자원봉사자들이 대부분의 자선 단체들의 중심을 이루고 있다.

341 mammoth
[mǽməθ]

a. 거대한
so exceedingly large

[syn] **huge, gigantic, vast** 거대한

This mammoth undertaking was completed in 18months.
이 대규모 사업은 18개월 만에 완성되었다.

342 expose
[ikspóuz]

v. 노출시키다
show; make visible

[syn] **display, show, exhibit** 전시하다, 나타내다　**disclose, divulge** 드러내다, 폭로하다

Soldiers found that an exposed site on the hill was the secret place of the enemy during the last war.
군인들은 언덕에 있는 한 공터가 지난 전쟁 당시 적군의 비밀 장소였음을 발견했다.

exposed adj. 드러나 있는　syn. uncovered
exposition n. 박람회, 전시회, 설명　syn.exhibition

343 from time to time

[syn] **now and then, occasionally, sometimes** 때때로, 종종

From time to time, inexact news on the fluctuation of current economy is likely to make many people confuse.
때때로 현재 경제 변동에 대한 부정확한 뉴스가 많은 사람들을 혼란스럽게 만드는 경향이 있다.

344 random
[rǽndəm]

a. 되는 대로의, 임의의, 무작위의
happening or done by chance

[syn] **accidental, haphazard, casual, arbitrary** 우연한, 임의의

The survey used the random sample of two thousand people across England and U.S.
그 조사는 영국과 미국 전역에서 무작위로 선정한 2천 명의 모집단을 사용했다.

Plus Data
in random 계획 없이 syn. without planning

345 **given**
[gívən]

a. 주어진, 정해진, 일정한
already decided, arranged, or agreed

syn **particular, specified, special** 특별한, 제한적인

About 250 students are working with us at any given time. 보통 약 250명의 학생들이 우리와 함께 일을 한다.

Plus Data
at any given time 보통, 평소

346 **particular**
[pərtikjulər]

a. 특별한, 특정한
special or this and not any other

syn **specific, special** 특정한, 특별한

Are there any particular topics that you would like me to explain further? 제 설명을 더 듣고 싶으신 점이 있으신가요?

particularly ad. 특히 syn. especially

347 **prophetic**
[prəfétik]

a. 예언의
foretelling events

syn **predictive, far-sighted** 예언의, 선견지명이 있는

His words proved oddly prophetic.
이상하게도 그의 말들이 예언적이라는 것이 증명되었다.

348 **object**
[ábdʒikt]

n. 목적, 물건, 물체
the goal intended to be attained; a material

v. 반대하다
feel or express opposition to or dislike of something or someone

syn **purpose, goal, aim** 목적 **thing, material** 사물ㅣ
oppose, disapprove 반대하다

The decision was made with the object of cutting costs.
그 결정은 경비를 삭감할 목적으로 내려졌다.

Plus Data

objective 객관적인 ↔ subjective 주관적인
objection n. 반대 syn. opposition

Word Root ▸ ject = throw

conjecture	v. 추측하다
deject	v. 슬프게 하다, 실망하다
ejaculate	v. 사출하다
inject	v. [액체, 약 따위를] 주사하다
interject	v. [말 따위를] 불쑥 끼워 넣다
project	v. 계획하다, 발사하다
reject	v. 거절하다
subject	n. 주제, 학과 v. 종속하다

349 refrain
[rifréin]

v. 삼가하다
not do something

syn **abstain** 삼가다 **limit, control, check, prohibit, prevent** 막다 **forbear** 참다 **pause** 멈추다

Please refrain from smoking in this area.
이 지역에서는 금연을 해 주십시오.

350 represent
[rèprizént]

v. 나타내다, 의미하다, 대표하다
serve as a means of expressing something; be representative

syn **stand for, symbolize** 상징하다 **characterize** 특징을 나타내다

Ambassador Albright will represent the United States at the ceremony. 올브라이트 대사가 그 행사에서 미국을 대표할 것이다.

351 robust
[roubʌ́st]

a. 강건한, 늠름한, [사상·의지가] 확고한
physically strong; strong enough to withstand intellectual challenged

syn **strong, sturdy** 튼튼한 **vigorous** 정력적인

A robust economy makes the people feel so prosperous and proud. 튼튼한 경제는 사람들로 하여금 매우 번창하고 있다고 느끼게 하며 또 자부심을 느끼게 한다.

352 sizable
[sàizəbl]

a. 상당한 크기의, 꽤 많은
large in amount, extent, or degree

syn **measurable, considerable** 상당한 **great, vast, enormous, huge, gigantic** 커다란

He earned a more sizable income than his friends because of his energetic devotion to his job. 그는 자신의 일에 열정적으로 헌신했기 때문에 그의 친구들보다 훨씬 많은 보수를 벌었다.

353 standpoint
[stǽndpɔint]

n. 관점
mental position from which things are considered or judged

syn **perspective, viewpoint** 관점, 견해

From a saver standpoint, high interest rates are a good thing. 저축하는 사람의 입장에서 보면, 높은 이자율은 좋은 것이다.

354 swell
[swel]

v. 부풀다, 팽창하다
become larger and rounder than usual; increase in size or amount

syn **expand, increase in size, bulge** 부풀다

When it rains in the morning, moisture causes the timber to swell. 아침에 비가 내리면, 수분은 목재를 부풀게 한다.

355 unbridled
[ʌnbràidld]

a. 억제되지 않은
not restrained or controlled

syn **unrestrained** 억제되지 않은 **unrestricted** 제한[구속]이 없는

The spokesperson spoke with unbridled passion.
그 대변인은 열정을 억제하지 않고 말했다.

bridle v. 삼가다, 저지하다 syn. check, curb, restrain

356 weariness
[wíərinis]

n. 피로
the state of being tired
syn **fatigue** 피로, 노고

He showed absolutely no signs of weariness.
그는 전혀 피곤한 기색을 보이지 않았다.

weary a. 지친 syn. tired, exhausted
wearisome a. 지치게 하는, 피곤하게 하는 syn. boring, dull, tedious, burdensome, fatiguing, tiresome

357 transfer
[trǽnsfɔ́ːr]

n. 이전, 환승
the act of transferring

v. 옮기다, 전입하다
move from one place to another

syn **relocation** 재배치 **transmission** 전달 | **convey** 운반하다 **move, shift** 이동하다

We're currently dealing with the paperwork for your transfer. 우리는 현재 당신의 전근에 관한 문서 업무를 하고 있습니다.

Word Root	▸ fer = carry
confer	v. 주다, 모으다
defer	v. 연기하다, 늦추다
differ	v. 의견이 다르다
indifferent	a. 무관심한, 냉담한
infer	v. 추리, 추론하다
interfere	v. 간섭, 참견하다
offer	v. 제공하다
prefer	v. 오히려 ~을 택하다, 좋아하다 [pre=before]
refer	v. 언급, 암시하다
suffer	v. [고통 따위를] 입다, 겪다
fertile	a. [토지 따위가] 비옥한

358 trigger
[trígər]

v. 유발하다
cause something bad start

syn **stimulate** 자극하다 **activate** 촉발하다

Further violence was triggered by the news of his death. 그의 사망 소식이 전해지자 더 큰 폭력이 촉발되었다.

359 withstand
[wiðstǽnd]

v. 저항하다, [물건들이 마찰 등에] 견디다
oppose with force or resolution

syn **resist** 저항하다 **tolerate, bear, endure, stand** 견디다

The bunker is designed to withstand a nuclear blast. 그 벙커는 핵폭발을 견딜 수 있도록 설계되었다.

360 secure
[sikjúər]

v. 안전하게 하다, 보장하다, 확보하다
guard from danger or risk of loss; make certain; get possession of

syn **make safe** 안전하게 하다 **guarantee** 보장하다 **obtain** 얻다

In September 1783, the Treaty of Paris secured American independence on generous terms.

1783년 9월 파리 조약은 관대한 조건으로 미국의 독립을 보장했다.

Review

☐ prophetic _____

☐ object _____

☐ refrain _____

☐ represent _____

☐ sizable _____

☐ robust _____

☐ particular _____

☐ standpoint _____

☐ unbridled _____

☐ secure _____

☐ swell _____

☐ trigger _____

☐ transfer _____

☐ withstand _____

☐ weariness _____

☐ potential _____

☐ significant _____

☐ propose _____

☐ renowned _____

☐ aim _____

☐ vanish _____

☐ sturdy _____

☐ classify _____

☐ mammoth _____

☐ territorial _____

☐ given _____

☐ from time to time _____

☐ random _____

☐ expose _____

☐ backbone _____

361–390

361 stunning
[stʌ́niŋ]

a. 근사한, 놀랄 만큼 아름다운
strikingly beautiful or attractive

syn **dramatic, excellent, astonishing** 놀라운

The view from the top of the hill is stunning.
언덕 꼭대기에서 본 광경은 정말 멋지다.

362 constituent
[kənstítʃuənt]

n. 구성 요소, 성분
a part of something

syn **component, element, factor** 구성 요소

The main constituents of wine are acid, tannin, alcohol, and sugar. 포도주의 주요 성분은 산, 타닌, 알코올과 설탕이다.

363 descent
[disént]

n. ① 가계, 혈통
the kinship relationship; the descendants of one individual
② 하강
a movement down

syn **origin** 출신 **falling** 하강

They're all of Irish descent. 그들은 모두 아일랜드계 혈통을 가지고 있다.

descendant n. 후손 syn. offspring, posterity, progeny

Word Root　　▶ scend, scan, scent = climb

ascend	v. 오르다 [a=up]
condescend	v. 겸손하게 자세를 낮추다 [con=together], [de=down]
transcend	v. 초월하다 [trans=pass]
transcendent	a. 뛰어난
transcendental	a. 초자연적인
transcendentalism	n. 초월주의, 선험주의

364 promote
[prəmóut]

v. 진행시키다
contribute to the progress or growth of

syn **further, advance** 진행시키다 **boost, elevate, upgrade** 향상시키다

A college course can help you find work or get promoted.
대학 과정은 당신이 직업을 찾거나 승진하는 데 도움이 된다.

promoting a. 향상, 진급된 syn. furthering

365 **debatable**
[dibéitəbl]

a. 논쟁의 여지가 있는
open to argument or debate

syn **questionable, controversial** 논쟁의 여지가 있는
doubtful, dubious 의심스러운

A debatable issue on air pollution of large cities causes
the government to try to find the solution of this problem.
대도시들의 공기 오염에 관한 논란의 여지가 있는 문제 때문에 정부에서는 그 해결책
을 찾기 위해 애쓰고 있다.

debated a. 논의된 syn. argued

366 **predominantly**
[pridámənəntli]

ad. 대개, 주로
much greater in number or influence

syn **primarily, chiefly, mainly** 대개, 주로

The women employed in the mills were predominantly
young and unmarried.
제분소에 고용된 여성들은 대개 젊은 미혼 여성들이었다.

predominant a. 압도적인, 지배적인 syn. prevailing, prevalent,
overwhelming

367 **severe**
[səvíər]

a. 엄격한, 심각한
very bad in degree or quality; unsparing and uncompromising
in discipline or judgment

syn **harsh, stern, rough, grave** 가혹한, 엄격한, 거친, 중대한

Overcrowding in Californian schools is pretty severe.
캘리포니아 학교들에 있어서 인구 과밀은 매우 심각하다.

368 **terrestrial**
[təréstriəl]

a. 지구(상)의, 육지의, 육상의
of or relating to the land; operating or living or growing on the
land

syn **territorial** 토지의 | **land** 육지

Although they can swim, polar bears are terrestrial
animals. 북극곰들은 비록 수영을 할 수는 있지만 육상 동물이다.

369 recur
[rikə́:r]

v. 재발하다, 회상하다

happen again; return in thought or speech to something

syn **return** 재발하다, 되돌아가다 **reappear** 재발하다, 다시 나타나다

We must make sure that the problem does not recur.
우리는 확실히 그 문제가 재발하지 않도록 해야 한다.

recurred a. 재발된 syn. returned
recurrence n. 재발

Word Root	► cur = run
concur	v. 동시에 일어나다
incur	v. 자초하다, 초래하다
occur	v. 일어나다, 발생하다
current	a. 현재의 n. 흐름, 경향, 추세

370 active
[ǽktiv]

a. 활동적인, 활동중인

characterized by energetic activity; taking part in operation

syn **lively** 활기찬 **brisk, nimble, agile** 민첩한

He is an active member of the American Cancer Society.
그는 미국암협회에서 할발하게 활동하고 있는 회원이다.

activity n. 활동 syn. capacity

371 annually
[ǽnjuəli]

ad. 일년마다

syn **yearly** 매년

Baku, the capital of Azerbaijan pumps some 250 to 300 million cubic meters of sewage into the Caspian annually.
아제르바이잔의 수도인 바쿠는 매년 약 2억 5천만에서 3억 입방미터의 오수를 카스피 해로 내보낸다.

Word Root	► ann = year
annual	a. 일년의
semiannual	a. 반년마다의
anniversary	n. 해마다 돌아오는 기념일
biennial	a. 2년마다의 bi - 2
decennial	a. 10년마다의 dece - 10
centennial	a. 100년마다의 cente - 100
bicentennial	a. 200년마다의 bicente - 200
perennial	a. 계속되는 per – 계속

372 budding
[bʌ́diŋ]

a. 싹트기 시작한, 세상에 갓 진출한, 유망한

beginning to develop; being like a bud in respect to youth and freshness or growth and promise

syn **emerging** 최근 생겨난 **promising** 유망한 **newly successful** 갓 성공한

The mangrove tree is in bud already.

맹그로브 나무는 벌써 움을 틔웠다.

bud v. 싹트다, 움트다, 꽃피우다   syn. sprout, blossom, burgeon
n. 싹, 움

373 congestion
[kəndʒéstʃən]

n. 혼잡

excessive crowding

syn **overcrowding** 혼잡

Traffic congestion and pollution are the main problems in modern city life. 교통 혼잡과 공해가 현대 도시 생활의 주요 문제들이다.

Word Root	▶ gest = carry
ingest	v. [음식물 등을] 섭취하다
digest	v. 소화하다
register	n. 기록부, 등록 v. 기록하다
suggest	v. 제안하다, 암시하다

374 dramatic
[drəmǽtik]

a. 극적인, 연극의

sensational in appearance or thrilling in effect; relating to plays and acting

syn **radical, drastic, extreme** 극적인 **impressive, spectacular** 인상적인 **theatrical** 연극의, 연극 같은

The change in him was dramatic. 그에게 일어난 변화는 극적이었다.

dramatically ad. 극적으로   syn. radically, severely

375 dense
[dens]

a. 조밀한, 진한

thick; closely crowded together; hard to go or see through

syn **thick, heavy, dark, intense** 조밀한, 두꺼운, 짙은

In the middle of the U.S, a dense black cloud of flying insects sometimes causes many people to remember the disaster of locusts. 미국 중부에서는 두꺼운 검은 구름처럼 날아다니는 곤충들이 때때로 많은 사람들에게 메뚜기 재앙을 생각나게 한다.

376 cease
[si:s]

v. 끝을 내다
put an end to a state or an activity

syn stop, finish, die down 그치다, 죽다

The rain had almost ceased by the time we left.
비는 우리가 떠날 즈음에 거의 그쳤다.

ceaseless a. 끊임없는 syn. endless, unending, perpetual, permanent

377 require
[rikwàiər]

v. 요구하다
need or make necessary

syn need, demand, call for 요구하다

Working with children requires a great deal of patience.
아이들과 함께 일하는 것은 많은 참을성을 요구한다.

required a. 의무적인, 강제의 syn. necessary, compulsory

378 rupture
[rʌ́ptʃər]

n. 파열
the instance of breaking open or bursting

syn burst, breaking 파열 **breach** 틈

A loud explosion caused them a rupture of the eardrum in the firework's factory last night.
지난 밤 불꽃 화약 공장에서 일어난 대형 폭발로 그들의 고막이 파열되었다.

379 govern
[gʌ́vərn]

v. 통치하다, 지배하다
exercise authority over

syn control, rule, direct, monitor 지배하다, 감독[관리]하다

The region is now governed by Morocco.
그 지역은 이제 모로코에 의해 통치되고 있다.

380 hail
[heil]

v. 환호하다
greet enthusiastically or joyfully

syn acclaim, applaud 환호하다, 박수 갈채하다

The court's ruling was immediately hailed as a victory for freedom. 법원의 판결은 자유에 대한 승리로 즉각 갈채를 받았다.

> **Plus Data**
> bombardment, shower 해일, 폭우, 강타 hailstone 우박

381 inadequate
[inǽdikwət]

a. 부적당한, 불충분한
not sufficient to meet a need

syn deficient, insufficient, lacking 부족한

We are trying to provide basic education with inadequate resources.
우리는 부족한 재원으로 기본적인 교육을 제공하기 위해 노력하고 있다.

382 unwitting
[ʌnwítiŋ]

a. 의식하지 않은, 부지중의
not aware or intentional; lacking information or knowledge

syn unintentional, without knowing 고의가 아닌
unconscious 무의식적인 **accidental** 우연의

Many parents unwittingly place their children in danger by not making sure they wear seat belts.
많은 부모들이 아이들이 안전벨트를 착용하는 것을 확실히 하지 않음으로써 부지중에 아이들을 위험에 방치한다.

383 manipulation
[mənìpjuléiʃən]

n. 조정, 조작
the act of controlling something using hands; exerting influence skillfully to one advantage

syn alteration 변경, 개조 **treatment** 가공, 처리

Scientists are attempting, by genetic manipulation, to produce more effective vaccines.
과학자들이 유전자 조작을 통해 더 효과적인 백신을 만들려고 시도하고 있는 중이다.

manipulate v. 교묘하게 다루다 syn. handle, manage

384 mounting
[máuntiŋ]

a. 점차 오르는
gradually increasing

syn increasing, rising, growing, escalating 오르는

There is mounting evidence of serious effects on people's health. 사람들의 건강에 미치는 심각한 영향에 대한 증거가 늘어나고 있다.

Plus Data
mounted a. 설치한, 끼워 박은 a ceiling-mounted fan 천장에 설치된 환풍기

385 occasion
[əkéiʒən]

n. 경우, 사건
the time of a particular event; a vaguely specified social event

[syn] **event** 사건, 경우

On one occasion we had to walk all the way home.
언젠가 우리는 집까지 줄곧 걸어야만 했다.

occasional a. 종종 syn. infrequent, irregular, sporadic

386 phase
[feiz]

n. 단계, 국면
any distinct time period or stage in a sequence of events or in a process of development

[syn] **period, stage** 국면

The war was about to enter its final phase.
전쟁은 마지막 국면으로 접어들고 있었다.

387 progressive
[prəgrésiv]

a. 진진하는, 침침직인
gradually advancing in extent

[syn] **continuous, ongoing** 지속적인 **increasing** 조금씩 증가하는 **gradual** 점진적인

The disease causes progressive deterioration of the nervous system. 그 병은 신경계의 점진적인 악화를 일으킨다.

progressively ad. 점차적으로 syn. increasingly

388 lucid
[lú:sid]

a. 명쾌한, 알기 쉬운
[of language] clear and easily understandable

[syn] **plain, articulate** 분명한, 표현이 명료한 **rational** 합리적인 **lucent** 반짝이는

His prose is always lucid and compelling.
그의 글은 항상 명쾌하며, 사람의 마음을 끌어 들인다.

389 especially
[ispéʃəli]

ad. 특히, 특별하게
to a distinctly greater degree than in common; in a special manner

[syn] **specifically, particularly** 특히 **notably** 현저하게

It was a very cold house, especially in the winter.
그 집은 겨울에는 몹시 추운 집이었다.

390 **far-reaching**
[fáːríːtʃiŋ]

a. 광범위한, 포괄적인
having bread range or effect

syn broad, far-embracing, extensive, comprehensive
넓은, 포괄적인 **general** 일반적인

The principal made a far-reaching statement on the problem of our circumstances in the morning. 아침에 교장은 우리가 처해 있는 상황의 문제점에 대해 광범위한 성명을 발표했다.

Review

☐ especially

☐ rupture

☐ hail

☐ require

☐ mounting

☐ stunning

☐ govern

☐ unwitting

☐ occasion

☐ dense

☐ manipulation

☐ lucid

☐ progressive

☐ budding

☐ phase

☐ far-reaching

☐ descent

☐ constituent

☐ inadequate

☐ predominantly

☐ recur

☐ severe

☐ debatable

☐ active

☐ terrestrial

☐ congestion

☐ promote

☐ annually

☐ dramatic

☐ cease

391-420

---

391 **short-lived**
[ʃɔːrt-lívd]

a. 수명이 짧은
enduring a very short time

syn brief, fleeting, passing, transient, transitory, temporary 짧은, 덧없는, 일시적인 **ephemeral** 단명의, 순식간의

Such a star would be very short-lived, but the magnetic fields inside it would be astounding.
그런 별은 수명이 매우 짧지만, 그 안에 있는 자기장은 아주 대단하다.

Plus Data
permanent(↔ short-lived) a. 영구적인

---

392 **sort**
[sɔːrt]

n. 종류
a group of things sharing similar qualities

syn type, variety, kind, class 종류

What sort are you looking for? 어떤 종류를 찾고 계십니까?

I need to sort out the mess on my desk.
나는 책상 위에 있는 지저분한 것들을 정리할 필요가 있다.

sort out v. 가려내다, 구별하다, 분류하다 syn. classify, separate, rank, arrange

---

393 **stretch**
[stretʃ]

v. 늘이다
make long or longer by pulling

syn extend, span, elongate, widen, broaden, enlarge 늘이다, 확장하다

I'll have to get these shoes stretched.
나는 이 신발을 늘여야만 할 것이다.

---

394 **unequal**
[ʌníːkwəl]

a. 부당한
poorly balanced or matched in quantity, value, or measure

syn unfair, uneven 부당한 **asymmetrical** 비대칭의, 불균형의 **inadequate** 적당치 못한

The women claimed they were given unequal treatment.
그 여자들은 자신들이 부당한 대우를 받고 있다고 주장했다.

unequaled a. 뛰어난, 비길 데 없는 syn. incomparable, unrivaled, unsurpassed, unmatched, superior

395 purify
[pjúərəfài]

v. 정화하다
remove bad substances from something to make it pure

syn **cleanse, sanitize** 깨끗하게 하다, 위생 처리하다

The rooms are equipped with systems that purify the air and water. 그 방들은 공기와 물을 정화하는 설비가 갖추어져 있다.

purified a. 정화된 syn. cleansed

396 replace
[ripléis]

v. 대신하다, 대리하다
take the place of

syn **substitute, take the place of, displace** 대체하다, 대리하다 **supersede** 대리하다 **supplant** 찬탈하다, [사물을] 대체하다

E-mail has largely replaced the traditional business letter.
이메일은 전통적인 비즈니스 서신을 대부분 대체해 나가고 있다.

397 symmetrical
[simétrikəl]

a. 대칭적인, 균형잡힌
having similarity in size, shape, and relative position of corresponding parts

syn **proportioned, balanced** 비례하는, 균형잡힌

The front of the church is completely symmetrical.
그 교회의 정면은 완전히 좌우대칭이다.

symmetry n. 조화, 대칭 syn. balance, correspondence, harmony, proportion

398 tendency
[téndənsi]

n. 경향, 추세, 풍조
a likelihood to do something

syn **trend** 추세, 경향 **inclination, disposition** 성향 **preference** 선호

There is a tendency for a new manager to make changes.
지배인이 새로 오면 변화가 있기 마련이다.

399 uniform
[júːnəfɔːrm]

a. 한결같은, 똑같은
showing a single form or character

syn **consistent, unvarying, regular, identical, alike** 변함없는, 비슷한 **homogeneous** 균질의

The staffs are uniformly polite and cheerful.
사원들이 한결같이 정중하고 명랑하다.

uniformly ad. 균등하게, 고르게 syn. evenly

400 as a result of

syn **due to, owing to** 때문에 **by means of** ~에 의해서 **as a consequence of** ~의 결과로

As a result of the 1990 census, the average size of a congressional district grew to about 572,000 people.
1990년 인구 조사 결과에 의하면, 의회 지역구의 평균 크기는 대략 572,000명으로 늘어났다.

401 aesthetic
[esθétik]

a. 심미적인, 예술의
of or concerning the appreciation of beauty or good taste; artistic

syn **artistic** 예술적인, 심미적인

The design is not particularly aesthetic, but at least it is practical. 그 디자인은 특별히 예술적이진 않지만 적어도 실용적이다.

aesthetically ad. 예술적으로 syn. artistically

402 abstract
[æbstrǽkt]

a. 추상적인
existing in the mind, not as a material object

syn **theoretical, conceptual, intangible** 추상적인

The direction of her work changed in Three Lives, where, in the central story, "Melanctha," Stein began to develop her characteristically abstract style.
스타인의 작품의 방향은 〈세 가지 삶〉에서 바뀌었다. 이 이야기에서 특히 중심적 이야기인 "Melanctha"에서 그녀의 특유한 추상체를 발전시키기 시작했다.

Plus Data
concrete(↔ abstract) a. 구체적인, 사실적인 syn. factual

403 **breeding**
[brí:diŋ]

n. 양육
raising of offspring

syn **reproduction** 번식 **upbringing** 양육 **ancestry, extraction, lineage** 가계, 혈통

The tiny animal is the result of generations of selective breeding. 그 작은 동물은 여러 세대에 걸친 선택적 번식의 결과이다.

404 **collect**
[kəlékt]

v. 모으다, 모이다
assemble or get together

syn **gather, assemble, accumulate** 모으다

People refer to these different medical conditions collectively as heart disease.
사람들은 이러한 다양한 질병 현상들을 모두 가리켜 심장병이라고 부른다.

collecting n. 모임, 집회 syn. gathering, group
collectively ad. 함께 syn. together

405 **correspondence**
[kɔ̀:rəspándəns]

n. 일치, 조화, 상응, 통신
the act, fact or state of agreeing; similarity; communication by exchanging of letters

syn **association** 연상 **resemblance, similarity** 유사함 **communication** 대화 **agreement** 일치

She kept up a thirty-year correspondence with Mary Hays.
그녀는 메리 헤이즈와 30년 동안 연락을 해왔다.

correspond v. 연락하다, 일치하다, 조화하다 syn. communicate, keep in touch with, match
correspondingly ad. 일치하게 syn. similarly

406 **direct**
[dirékt]

v. ~을 향하다, 명령하다
aim at; be in charge of

syn **aim, order, manage** 목표하다, 관리[지배, 통제]하다 | **straight, exact** 곧바른, 정확한

A new manager has been appointed to direct the project.
그 프로젝트를 진행하기 위해 새 매니저가 임명되었다.

directed a. 인도된, 맞춰진 syn. guided, focusing on

407 eradicate
[irǽdəkèit]

v. 전멸하다, 제거하다
destroy completely

syn **eliminate, wipe out, get rid of** 제거하다

Inflation will never be completely eradicated from the economy. 인플레이션은 경제로부터 결코 완벽하게 제거되지 않을 것이다.

408 expand
[ikspǽnd]

v. 확장하다
become larger in size, number, or importance

syn **increase, enlarge, inflate, spread out** 확장하다

The water froze inside the pipe, causing it to expand and burst. 파이프 안에 물이 얼어붙었는데, 파이프를 팽창시켜 터지게 만들었다.

409 fine
[fain]

a. ① 좋은 ② 가느다란 ③ 미세한, 고운 ④ 뛰어난
become larger in size, number, or importance

syn **tiny, thin, minute, subtle** 작은, 가는, 세밀한, 섬세한

Everything was covered in a fine layer of dust.
모든 것이 얇은 먼지 층으로 덮여 있었다.

finely ad. 세세히, 세밀히, 멋지게 syn. minutely

410 incessant
[insésnt]

a. 끊임없는
occurring so frequently as to seem ceaseless or uninterrupted

syn **unceasing, constant, unending, endless, permanent, perpetual** 끊임없는, 계속되는, 영속하는

Incessant rain made conditions almost intolerable.
계속되는 비가 상황을 거의 견딜 수 없게 만들었다.

Plus Data
temporary a.일시적인 syn. transient, fleeting, prudent

411 mask
[mæsk]

v. 가리다, 감추다
prevent something from being seen or noticed

syn **disguise, camouflage** 위장시키다 **cover, conceal** 감추다

His blue eyes were masked by dark glasses.
그의 파란 눈은 짙은 색의 안경에 가려져 있었다.

412 negligible
[néglidʒəbl]

a. 하찮은, 대수롭지 않은
not worth considering; so small as to be meaningless

syn **insignificant, unimportant** 중요하지 않은 **trivial, trifle, minimal** 사소한

In these days of Great Depression, Government could not make a negligible rise in employment at all.
대공황 당시에, 정부는 고용율을 눈곱만큼도 높일 수가 없었다.

413 partially
[páːrʃəli]

ad. 부분적으로
in part; in some degree; not whole

syn **incompletely, partly, to some extent** 부분적으로

The airline is partially owned by British Airways.
그 항공사는 British Airways 가 부분적으로 소유하고 있다.

> **Plus Data**
> impartial(↔ partial) a. 공정한, 편견이 없는 syn. just, unbiased

414 profitable
[práfitəbl]

a. 유익한, 이익이 되는
productive; of profit

syn **advantageous, gainful, lucrative** 유리한, 이익이 되는

Some of their new electronic products are highly profitable.
새로운 전자 제품들 중에 몇 개는 이윤이 매우 높다.

415 raw
[rɔː]

a. 날것의, 가공되지 않은
not cooked; not processed; in a natural state

syn **unprocessed, uncooked, rude** 가공되지 않은 **crude**
천연의

Sashimi is a Japanese dish of raw fish cut into very thin slices. 사시미는 날 생선을 매우 얇은 조각으로 썰어 내는 일본 음식이다.

416 trace
[treis]

n. 자취, 흔적
a sign that something has been present
v. 추적하다, 거슬러 올라가다
follow the course or trail of

syn **imprint** 흔적 **residue** 잔여 | **find, locate, pursue, track** 추적하다 **draw, map out, outline, sketch** 그리다, 생각하다

Detectives have so far failed to trace the missing woman.
탐정들은 지금까지 그 사라진 여자를 추적하는 데 실패했다.

417 subject
[sʌ́bdʒikt]

a. 영향을 받는
being under the power of

v. 종속[복종]시키다
make someone submit to the authority of

[syn] **susceptible, prone, vulnerable** 영향 받기 쉬운 | **submit, control, dominate** 종속[복종]시키다, 지배하다

He is subject(=susceptible) to fits of anger.
그는 울컥 화를 내는 경향이 있다.

The strong Roman Empire subjected(=dominated) most areas by using force.
막강 로마 제국은 무력으로 대부분의 지역을 정복했다.

subjective a. 주관적인, 사적인 syn. personal, biased
objective a. 객관적인 ant. impartial, unbiased

Plus Data
theme, topic 주제 study 학과목

418 stealthily
[stélθili]

ad. 몰래, 은밀히
in a manner marked by quiet, caution, and secrecy

[syn] **silently** 조용히 **secretly, covertly** 비밀리에

Slowly and stealthily, someone was creeping up the stairs. 천천히 그리고 은밀하게 누군가가 층계를 기어올라가고 있었다.

419 terminate
[tə́ːrmənèit]

v. 끝내다, 종결하다
bring to a conclusion; cause to come to an end

[syn] **finish, stop, come to an end, expire, end** 끝나다

The military operation was terminated in 1969.
그 군사 작전은 1969년에 끝났다.

Word Root   ▸ termin = end, limit, boundary
exterminate   v. 근절하다 [ex=out]
determine   v. 결정하다, 결심하다 [de=away]
interminable   a. 지루한, 끝임없는 [in=not]
terminal   n. 터미널
terminology   n. 전문 용어

420 **restrict**
[ristríkt]

v. 제한하다, 한정하다
place limits on

[syn] **limit, control, check** 제한하다, 저지하다, 억제하다 **impede, hamper** 방해하다

Travel is a dream of mine, but a busy working life has restricted my opportunities.
여행은 나의 꿈이다, 그러나 바쁜 일상이 기회를 막아버린다.

restricted a. 제한된 syn. **restrained**

Review

□ expand

□ direct

□ eradicate

□ fine

□ unequal

□ stealthily

□ mask

□ negligible

□ profitable

□ partially

□ raw

□ trace

□ subject

□ terminate

□ restrict

□ correspondence

□ stretch

□ short-lived

□ sort

□ purify

□ breeding

□ tendency

□ as a result of

□ uniform

□ symmetrical

□ incessant

□ aesthetic

□ abstract

□ collect

□ replace

421-450

421 **type**
[taip]

n. 유형

a group of people or things which shares similar characteristics and forms

[syn] **form, kind, style, variety, sort, category** 형태, 종류

Adobes were the typical residence types in the United States. 어도비 벽돌집은 미국의 전형적인 주택 형태였다.

422 **unqualified**
[ʌnkwálɔfàid]

a. 자격 미달의, 무조건의

not meeting the proper standards and requirements; not limited or restricted

[syn] **untrained, unskilled, incompetent** 자격 미달의 **complete** 무조건의, 전적인

You have my unqualified support in this matter.
이 문제에 있어서 당신은 나의 무조건적인 지지를 받고 있습니다.

423 **wear**
[wɛər]

v. ① 해지게 하다

become weaker or damaged through continuous use

② 입다

have clothing or else on your body

[syn] **use, rub out** 써서 닳게 하다 **put on** 입다

The carpet has worn very thin in places.
카페트는 곳곳이 닳아서 매우 얇아졌다.

424 **full**
[ful]

a. 충분한

complete in extent or degree

[syn] **filled, extensive, complete** 가득 찬, 광범위한, 전부의, 완벽한

A full report on this research will appear in the October 1 issue of Geophysical Research Letters.
이 연구에 대한 완전한 보고서가 Geophysical Research Letters(지구 물리학 연구 레터) 10월 1일 호에 발표될 것이다.

425 **prolong**
[prəlɔ́ːŋ]

v. 연장하다, 확장하다
lengthen or extend in duration or space

syn **extend, lengthen, protract** 확장하다 **delay, put off** 연기하다

The ongoing violence has prolonged the suffering of our people. 계속되는 폭력이 우리 국민의 고통을 연장시키고 있다.

prolonged a. 길어진 syn. extended, expanded

426 **remedy**
[rémədi]

v. 교정하다, 치료하다, 해결하다
set straight or right; provide relief for

n. 치료, 구제책, 배상
a successful way of curing an illness or dealing with a problem or difficulty

syn **correct, cure, solve** 고치다, 치료하다, 해결하다

The bill seeks to remedy a historic injustice in which blacks were deprived of their right to own lands.
그 법안은 흑인들이 토지 소유권을 박탈당했던 역사적 불평등을 바로 잡으려는 것이다.

427 **stock**
[stɑk]

v. [상품 등을] 비축하다
provide with goods

n. 재고품, 비축, 저장
a supply of something for use or sale

syn **furnish, provision, supply, carry** 공급하다 | **inventory, merchandise, reserve, store** 저장, 축적

They had stocked their refrigerator with plenty of food before the big game.
그들은 그 중요한 경기가 시작되기 전에 많은 음식을 냉장고에 채워 넣었다.

428 **supremacy**
[səprémǝsi]

n. 우월, 우위
power to dominate

syn **dominancy, preeminence, superiority, primacy** 우월

Rival gangs battled for supremacy in their area.
경쟁 관계에 있는 갱들이 그들 지역에서의 우위를 놓고 싸웠다.

429 **excluding**
[iksklú:diŋ]

prep. ~을 제외하고

[syn] **without, not including, other than, except, but** 제외하고

The average cost, excluding insurance, is around $600 a year. 보험을 제외한 평균 비용은 1년에 대략 600불 입니다.

Plus Data

exclusively ad. 배타적인 syn. selectively, restrictively
exclusive a. 홀로, 단독의 syn. sole, alone

Word Root ▶ clude = shut

exclude	v. 배제하다, 빼다 [ex=out]
conclude	v. 결론짓다 [con=together]
include	v. 포함하다
seclude	v. 격리시키다, 은퇴하다 [se=away, apart]
preclude	v. 막다, 방해하다 [pre=before]

430 **cardinal**
[ká:rdənl]

a. 중요한
of great importance

[syn] **important, fundamental, essential, chief**
중요한, 근본적인

The cardinal rule in working with large powerful animals is never to take any risks. 크고 힘이 센 동물들을 다루는 데 있어서 중요한 규칙은 절대로 위험한 일은 시도하지 않는 것이다.

431 **adhere**
[ædhíər]

v. 달라붙다, 고수하다
stick to firmly; follow through or carry cut a plan without deviation

[syn] **stick, cling, hold, stay** 달라붙다, 머물다

We must strictly adhere to the terms of the contract.
우리는 계약 조건을 엄격하게 고수해야만 합니다.

adhesion n. 부착, 접착력

Word Root ▶ her = stick

cohere	v. 밀착하다, 앞뒤 논리가 맞다
inhere	v. 타고나다
inherent	a. 고유한, 선천적인
inherit	v. 유산으로 물려주다
heritage	n. 유산
heredity	n. 유전

432 **comparable**
[kámpərəbl]

a. 비교할 수 있는, 공통점이 있는, 유사한, 동등한
able to be compared; similar or equivalent

syn **similar, identical, same, equal, equivalent**
비슷한, 같은, 상응하는

The two of them are in comparable financial situations.
그들 둘은 비슷한 재정 상황에 처해 있다.

comparative a. 상대적인 syn. relative

433 **concentrate**
[kánsəntrèit]

v. 집중하다
focus one attention on something

syn **focus on, give attention to, think over, contemplate** 집중하다, 곰곰이 생각하다

Stop talking and concentrate on your work.
그만 잡담하고 일에 집중해라.

concentration n. 집중, 농도 syn. density

434 **disperse**
[dispə́:rs]

v. 흩어지게 하다, 흩어지다
[cause to] move away from each other

syn **scatter, spread out, disseminate, dissipate**
흩뜨리다

Soldiers fired tear gas to disperse the crowds.
군인들은 무리를 해산 시키기 위해서 최루 가스를 발사했다.

435 **enter**
[éntər]

v. 들어가다
come or go into a particular place

syn **go into, come in** 들어가다

The man had entered through the back door.
그 사람은 뒷문으로 들어갔다.

436 **train**
[trein]

v. 훈련하다
exercise in order to prepare for an event or competition

syn **exercise** 훈련하다 **aim** 조준하다

You have to train yourself to stay calm.
침착하게 행동하도록 자기 자신을 훈련해야 한다.

training n. 교육, 훈련 syn. discipline, education, instruction

437 flexible
[fléksəbl]

a. 유연한, 융통성이 있는
able to bend easily; able to adjust readily to different conditions

syn **adaptable, plastic, elastic** 유연한

A more flexible approach to childcare arrangements is needed. 어린이 보육 제도에 대해 보다 융통성 있는 접근이 필요하다.

Plus Data
rigid(↔ flexible) a. 융통성 없는, 딱딱한 syn. stiff

438 fragrance
[fréigrəns]

n. 향기, 향기로움
sweet scent, sweetness of smell

syn **smell, scent, aroma** 향기, 향료

After arranging the garden, there remains the fragrance of freshly mowed grass.
정원을 정돈하고 나니 금방 깎은 잔디의 상쾌한 향기가 감돌았다.

fragrant a. 냄새가 좋은 syn. aromatic, perfumed

439 implement
[ímpləmənt]

n. 도구
a piece of equipment or tool used to
v. 행하다
put into practical effect

syn **tool, mechanism** 도구, 기계 | **carry out, apply, employ, put into practice** 이행하다, 실행하다

Attempts to implement changes have met with strong opposition. 변화를 일으키려는 시도들은 강한 반발에 부딪쳤다.

440 invaluable
[invǽljuəbl]

a. 값을 매길 수 없는, 매우 귀중한
valuable beyond estimation; priceless

syn **valuable, priceless, precious, essential, indispensable** 귀중한, 중요한

His experience of teaching in Mexico proved invaluable.
멕시코에서 교편을 잡았던 경험이 매우 귀중하다는 것을 알게 되었다.

441 range
[reindʒ]

n. 범위, 폭, 종류
a variety of things or activities
v. 배치하다, 변동[변화]하다

position people or things together; vary within specified limits

syn **variety, scope, sort** [변동의] 범위, 폭, 종류 I **vary, extend, stretch** 다양하다, 늘어놓다

We stock a wide range of office furniture.
우리는 다양한 종류의 사무 가구를 비축하고 있다.

442 swift
[swift]

a. 빠른, 신속한
moving very fast

syn **fast, quick, hasty, prompt** 빠른

The sea current was swift and dangerous.
해류는 빠르고 위험했다.

swiftly ad. 재빠르게 syn. quickly

443 thrive
[θraiv]

v. 번성하다, 부유해지다
grow stronger; gain in wealth

syn **prosper, flourish, bloom, blossom** 번성하다, 발전하다

Children thrive when given plenty of love and attention.
충분한 사랑과 관심을 기울이면 아이들은 발전한다.

444 meticulous
[mətíkjuləs]

a. 꼼꼼한, 정확한
giving extreme care in treatment of details

syn **careful, painstaking, detailed** 공들인, 세심한

Everyone agreed that it was a piece of meticulous research. 그것이 한 편의 공들인 연구라는 것에 모든 사람이 동의했다.

meticulously ad. 세심하게, 꼼꼼하게 syn. carefully

445 perspective
[pəːrspéktiv]

n. 관점, 조망, 통찰력
a particular way of considering something; the ability to perceive things in their importance

syn **viewpoint, attitude, perception** 관점, 태도, 통찰력

The book deals with a woman perspective on revolutionary change. 그 책은 혁신적인 변화에 대해 여성의 관점에서 다루고 있다.

Word Root	▸ spect = see
aspect	n. 양상, 국면
circumspect	a. 신중한, 주의 깊은 [circum=around]
expect	v. 기대하다, 예상하다
inspect	v. 검사[조사]하다
introspect	v. 내성, 자기 관찰하다 [intro=within]
respect	n. 존경, 경의 [re=again]
retrospect	n. 회고, 회상 [retro=backward]
suspect	v. 의심하다 [sus/sub=under]

446 owing to

syn **because of, due to, on account of, thanks to**
때문에, 덕분에

The mild shaking of distant regions can last hours, owing to the echoing of the seismic waves within the Earth.
먼 지역에서 발생한 경미한 흔들림도 지구 안에서의 지진파의 반향 때문에 몇 시간 동안 지속될 수 있다.

447 trivial
[tríviəl]

a. 하찮은, 사소한
small and of little importance

syn **unimportant, insignificant, trifling, minor, minimal** 중요하지 않은, 사소한

Why do they get so upset over such a trivial matter?
왜 그들은 그토록 사소한 문제에 대해 그렇게 실망하는가?

448 replica
[réplikə]

n. 사본, 복제
copy that is not the original; something that has been replicated

syn **copy, model, duplication, reproduction** 복사, 복제, 복사물, 복제물

They succeeded in building a replica of a 19th-century sailing ship. 그들은 19세기 범선의 복제품을 만들어내는 데 성공했다.

449 snatch
[snætʃ]

v. 잡아채다
grasp hastily or eagerly

syn **grab, grasp, seize** 손에 쥐다

Her brother snatched the letter and tore it open.
그녀의 동생은 그 편지를 확 낚아채더니 찢어서 개봉했다.

450 **sprawl**
[sprɔːl]

v. 불규칙하게 퍼지다

spread in a irregular way; sit or lie with one limbs spread out untidily

[syn] **stretch out, extend, spread out** 뻗치다, 퍼지다 | **stretch, expansion, sprawling movement** 확대, 팽창, 확장

As the large lake cities become more and more prosperous, they sprawled along the side of the lake.
그 큰 호수 주변의 도시들은 점점 더 번창하면서 호숫가를 따라 퍼져나갔다.

Review

□ invaluable _____

□ implement _____

□ perspective _____

□ train _____

□ thrive _____

□ swift _____

□ flexible _____

□ range _____

□ meticulous _____

□ owing to _____

□ sprawl _____

□ trivial _____

□ fragrance _____

□ replica _____

□ snatch _____

□ full _____

□ stock _____

□ concentrate _____

□ unqualified _____

□ type _____

□ supremacy _____

□ remedy _____

□ prolong _____

□ excluding _____

□ wear _____

□ cardinal _____

□ adhere _____

□ disperse _____

□ enter _____

□ comparable _____

자연 I
생태학, 환경, 기상학, 지질학, 해양학, 천문학

Ecology
생태학

biosphere 생물 영역

cambium 형성층

catalysis 촉매

conservationist (자연, 자원) 보호론자

consumer 소비자

crop pest 농작물 해

decomposer 분해자

deforestation 산림파괴

desertification 사막화

domestic 집에서 기른

dust storm 먼지 폭풍

ecological efficiency 생태 효율

ecosystem 생태계

endangered species 멸종 위기에 있는 생물

extinction 멸종

food chain 먹이사슬

food web 먹이그물

geothermal 지열의

geyser 간헐천

global warming 지구온난화

greenhouse effect 온실효과

habitat 서식지 = environment

hot spring 온천 = spa

humidity 습기

humus 부식토

noxious 유해한, 유독한

organism 유기체, 생물체

overpopulation 인구과잉

ozone hole 오존 구멍

pest 유해물, 해충

pesticide 살충제

photochemical smog 광화학 스모그

producer 생산자

purification 정화

rain forest 열대우림

reclamation 재개발, 개간

recycle 재활용하다

replant 다시 나무를 심다

runoff 빗물

tract (지면, 하늘 바다 등의) 넓이

wild life 야생동물

Environment
환경

acid precipitation 산성 강우(산성비를 포함한 큰 개념)

acid rain 산성비

air pollution 대기 오염

catastrophe 재앙, 재난

chemosynthesis 화학합성

garbage 쓰레기

landfill 쓰레기 매립지

oil spill 석유 유출

pollutant 오염 물질
reprocess 재생하다
salvage 폐품 수집
sewage 하수
soil contamination 토양 오염
untreated 정화되지 않은
waste water 폐수

Geology

지질학

Antarctic 남극의
archipelago 군도
Arctic 북극의
aurora 극광, 오로라
bulge 융기
canyon 협곡
cavern 큰 동굴
corrosion 부식, 침식
crust 지각
delta 삼각주
earthquake 지진
epicenter 진앙, 진원지
erosion 침식
glacier 빙하
granite 화강암
hot spring 온천
ice sheet 얼음판
iceberg 빙산
latitude 위도
lava 용암
limestone 석회암

longitude 경도
pangaea 판게아
plate tectonics 판구조론
river basin 유역
sand dune 사구
seismic intensity 지진 세기
stalactite 종유석
stalagmite 석순
subfrigid 아한대의
subtropical 아열대의
swamp 늪, 소택
tremor 진동
trench 해구
tributary (강의) 지류

Meteorology

기상학

aero logical diagram 기상도
atmosphere 대기
barometric pressure 기압
air mass 기단
atmosphere 대기
barometric pressure 기압
below freezing 영하
blizzard 눈보라
Celsius 섭씨
Fahrenheit 화씨
climate 기후
cold front 한랭전선
conservationist 환경 보호론자
continental climate 대륙성 기후

cumulus 적운

dew 이슬

drizzle 이슬비

frost 서리

geyser 간헐천

hail 우박

humidity 습도

icecap 만년설

meteorologist 기상학자

mist 엷은 안개

precipitation 강우

sleet 진눈깨비

summer solstice 하지

winter solstice 동지

squall 돌풍

torrential rain 호우

turbulence 난류

typhoon 태풍

warm front 온난전선

cold front 한랭전선

weather bureau 기상청

Oceanography
해양학

Antarctic Ocean 남극해

Arctic Ocean 북극해

Atlantic Ocean 대서양

circulation 순환

continental shelf 대륙붕

counterclockwise 반시계 방향으로

current 조류

gyre 회전, 소용돌이

Indian Ocean 인도양

mooring 계류, 정박

Northern Hemisphere 북반구

ocean floor 해저

Pacific Ocean 태평양

plain 평평한

plankton 플랑크톤

salinity 염도

submersible 잠수할 수 있는

tidal wave 해일

tide 조수

tsunami 해일

Astronomy
천문학

aerospace 우주공간, 항공우주과학

air resistance 공기 저항

antimatter 반물질

apogee 원지점(가장 먼 곳)

application satellite 실용 위성

asteroid 소행성

astrology 점성학

astronaut 우주비행사

astronautics 우주항공학

astronomer 천문학자

astronomical 천문의

atmosphere 대기

balloon satellite 기구위성

big bang 대폭발, 빅뱅

blackout 통신두절

blast-off (로켓 등의) 발사

broadcasting satellite 방송위성

canopy 하늘, 차양(햇볕가리개)

carrier rocket 운반 로켓

celestial sphere 천구

chromo sphere 채층(태양 주변의 백열 가스층)

circumlunar flight 달 궤도 비행

cluster 성단

combustion chamber (로켓의) 연소실

comet 혜성

constellation 성좌, 별자리

cosmology 우주론

density 밀도, 농도

detect 탐지하다

distance 거리

dust 먼지

eclipse 일식, 월식

fireball 불덩어리

friction 마찰

frozen 얼다

galaxy 성운, 은하

gravity 중력

Great Dipper 북두칠성

heavenly body 천체 = celestial body

Jupiter 목성

light-year 광년

luminous 빛을 내는

magnetic storm 자기 폭풍

Mars 화성

measure 측정하다

Mercury 수성

Meteor 유성

meteor 유성, 운석

Milky Way 은하계

naked eye 육안

nebular 성운

Neptune 해왕성

neutron star 중성자별

observatory 관측소

perigee 근지점(가장 가까운 지점)

planet 행성

planetology 행성학

Pluto 명왕성

proton 양성자

red giant star 적색거성

revolution 공전

revolve 자전하다

rotation 자전

Saturn 토성

solar system 태양계

stationary 정지된

stellar 별의

supernova 초신성

Uranus 천왕성

Variable Star 변광성

Venus 금성

white dwarf star 백색왜성

4th week

451-480

---

451 **abhor**
[æbhɔ́:r]

v. 혐오하다
to regard with horror or disgust; detest

[syn] **loathe, abominate, detest, dislike** 혐오하다

Martin Luther King **abhorred** the use of violence in any case. 마틴 루터 킹은 어떤 상황에서도 폭력 사용을 혐오했다.

---

452 **string**
[stríŋ]

n. 한 줄, 일련
a set of objects threaded together; a sequentially ordered set of things or ideas in which each successive member is related to the preceding

v. 묶다, 매달다
tie or fasten with a string

[syn] **series, sequence** 연속, 일련 | **tie, hang** 묶다, 매달다

He owns a **string** of restaurants in the Midwest.
그는 미국 중서부에 몇 개의 식당을 소유하고 있다.

---

453 **application**
[æ̀plikéiʃən]

n. [특정 목적·용도에] 적용, 응용
the act of using something for a purpose; [especially of rule or lows] having a connection or being important

[syn] **employment, use, association** 적용, 응용
connection, relevance, relationship 관련, 연관

This section of the law is **applicable** only to corporations.
이 법률 조항은 주식회사에만 적용된다.

applicable a. 적절한, 관련된   syn. appropriate, pertinent, related, relevant
apply v. 적용하다, 관련이 있다   syn. be relevant, pertain

Plus Data
apply oneself to, devote oneself to   ~에 기여하다, 헌신하다

454 bare
[bɛər]

a. 발가벗은, 노출된
not having a covering

syn **naked, uncovered, simple** 발가벗은, 단순한

Do not touch the stove with bare hands.
난로를 맨손으로 만지지 말아라.

455 capricious
[kəpríʃəs]

a. 변덕스러운
determined by chance or impulse or whim

syn **unpredictable, vagarious** 변덕스러운 **changeable, variable** 변하기 쉬운

A movie star who was capricious and difficult to please always made troubles with spectators.
변덕스럽고 까다로운 영화 배우 한 사람이 항상 관객과 문제를 일으켰다.

456 chamber
[tʃéimbər]

n. 방
a room; a natural or artificial enclosed space

syn **compartment, hall** 방, 구획

The council chamber of city hall is the place where committee meet in order to make a important decision.
시청의 회의실은 위원회가 중요한 결정을 내리기 위해 모이는 장소이다.

457 consort
[kánsɔːrt]

v. 사귀다, 교제하다
keep company with, hang out with, associate

syn **associate, socialize** 조화하다, 교제하다 | **mate, partner, spouse** 동료, 배우자

The American government was known to have consorted with Iraq secretly.
미국 정부가 이라크와 비밀리에 제휴했던 것이 알려졌다.

458 defeat
[difít]

v. 이기다
win a victory over

syn **conquer, beat, overcome, overwhelm** 정복하다, 극복하다, 압도하다

The Yankees defeated the Red Sox in the World Series.
양키스는 월드시리즈에서 레드삭스를 이겼다.

459 distribute
[distríbjuːt]

v. 분배하다, 골고루 퍼뜨리다
give shares of; spread about

syn allocate, allot, assign, dispense 분배하다 **spread out** 퍼뜨리다

Red squirrels are widely distributed throughout the woodlands. 빨간 다람쥐들이 숲에 널리 분포하고 있다.

distributed a. 분포된, 퍼진 syn. spread out, arrayed, diverse

Word Root	▶ tribut = give
attributes	n. 속성, 특질
attribute	v. ~에 기인하다
contribute	v. 기여[기부]하다
tributary	a. 공물을 바치는, 지류의

460 undertaking
[ʌ̀ndərtéikiŋ]

n. [일·책임의] 인수, 떠맡은 일
a task or assignment undertaken

syn task, responsibility, enterprise 일, 의무, 사업

In those days, the trip across country was a dangerous undertaking. 그 시절에 국토를 횡단하는 여행은 위험한 일이었다.

461 equivalent
[ikwívələnt]

a. 같은 가치[양]의, 상당하는
equal in amount or value; essentially equal

syn comparable, corresponding, equal, interchangeable 상응하는, 교환할 수 있는 | **counterpart** 상대편

The successful applicant will have a bachelor's or an equivalent degree.
지원 자격은 학사 또는 그에 상응하는 학위를 갖춘 사람이 될 것이다.

462 extant
[ekstǽnt]

a. 현존하는
still in existence; not extinct, destroyed, or lost

syn existing, present 존재하는

They found the extant remains of the ancient wall.
그들은 그 고대 성벽의 현존하는 유적을 발굴해 냈다.

Plus Data
extinct(↔ extant) a. 멸종된, 사라진

463 **fervor**
[fə́:rvər]

n. 열렬, 열정
feelings of great warmth and intensity

syn **zeal, passion, enthusiasm** 열정

Native Americans had the fervor in making tools of the agriculture. 미국 원주민들은 농기구를 만드는 데 심혈을 기울였다.

fervent a. 열정적인 syn. eager, passionate, ardent, avid, energetic, enthusiastic

464 **gather**
[gǽðər]

v. 모으다, 모이다
bring or come together

syn **collect, group, assemble, congregate, get together** 모이다

A crowd gathered outside the hotel.

군중들은 호텔 밖에 모여 있었다.

gathering n. 수집, 수집품, 수확물 syn. collecting, harvest

465 **pioneering**
[pàiəníəriŋ]

syn **initiating, original, new, ground-breaking, revolutionary** 시작하는, 독창적인, 새로운, 혁신적인

Through their hard pioneering experiments, they could get a good solution.

그들은 개척적인 고된 실험을 통해 좋은 결과를 얻을 수 있었다.

pioneer v. 개척하다(prepare or open a way for)

466 **be in charge of**

v. 책임을 맡다
having control over or responsibility for

syn **be responsible for, be entrusted with, be assigned to** 책임을 지다, 떠맡다

Philip is in charge of our marketing department.

Philip은 우리 마케팅 부서의 책임자이다.

467 **intend**
[inténd]

v. 의도하다, ~할 작정이다
to have in mind; plan

syn **aim, mean, expect, plan, direct a mind on**
의도하다, ~할 작정이다

The company intends a slow down in expansion.

회사는 확장 속도를 늦출 예정이다.

468 loom
[lu:m]

v. 어렴풋이 나타나다, 거대한 모습을 나타내다
come into view as a massive, distorted, or indistinct image

syn **become visible, appear, come out, emerge**
보이다, 나타나다

Suddenly the mountains loomed up out of the mist.
갑자기 안개 속에서 산이 나타났다.

469 manifestation
[mǽnəfistéiʃən]

n. 표명, 징후
a clear appearance, an indication of the presence of something

syn **demonstration, expression, sign, symptom**
증명[실연], 표현, 징후, 조짐

The demonstrations were a manifestation of the people's discontent. 그 집회들은 사람들의 불만의 표현이었다.

470 mediate
[mí:dièit]

v. 중재하다
act between parities with a view reconciling differences

syn **arbitrate, conciliate** 중재하다, 화해시키다 **negotiate**
협상하다 **influence** 영향을 끼치다

They mediated territorial disputes between neighboring nations. 그들은 이웃 국가들 간의 영토 분쟁을 중재했다.

> **Plus Data**
> meditate v. 명상하다, 숙고하다 syn. contemplate, deliberate, ponder, reflect, think

471 output
[àutpùt]

n. 생산물, 생산
things produced; the act or process of producing

syn **production, yield, harvest** 생산, 생산물

Industrial output increased by four percent last year.
산업 생산량은 작년에 4% 증가했다.

472 pressing
[présiŋ]

a. 긴급한, 절박한
demanding immediate attention; urgent

syn **urgent, vital, critical** 긴급한, 중요한

The safety of the hostages is a matter of pressing concern.
인질의 안전 문제는 긴급 사안이다.

press v. 누르다, 재촉하다   syn. push, pressure

473 provide
[prəváid]

v. 제공하다
furnish or supply; make available

syn **supply, present, offer, furnish** 제공하다

Our office can provide information on the local area.
우리 사무실은 지역 정보를 제공할 수 있다.

474 recently
[rí:sntli]

syn **lately, in these days, currently** 최근에
He has been back to America fairly recently.
그는 비교적 최근에 미국으로 돌아왔다.

475 relatively
[rélətivli]

ad. 상대적으로
in comparison with something else

syn **comparatively** 상대적으로 **somewhat, rather** 다소

Relatively few women become airline pilots.
상대적으로 여성 비행기 조종사는 거의 없다.

476 seek (out)
[si:k]

v. 찾다
look for a specific person or thing

syn **try to find, look for, search for** 찾다, 구하다

We can only guess why male butterflies seek these
territories. 우리는 왜 수나비가 이 지역을 찾는지는 오직 추측할 수 있을 뿐이다.

477 spot
[spɑt]

v. ① 발견하다
see or notice someone or something
② 더럽히다
cause a spot or spots appear on; cause a discoloration or
make a stain; disgrace
n. 점, 지점, 얼룩
a particular place, a stain

syn **see, notice** 발견하다, 분간하다 **stain** 얼룩지게 하다, [명예를]
더럽히다 **tarnish** 녹슬게 하다, 변색시키다, [명예를] 더럽히다 | **mark,
point** 표시 **location, place** 장소 **stain** 얼룩

Mara spotted the book she gave Ed for his birthday in the trash. 마라는 그녀가 에드에게 생일 선물로 준 책을 휴지통에서 발견했다.

478 **taboo**
[təbúː]

a. 금지된
excluded from use or mention

n. 금지
a ban or inhibition resulting from social custom

v. 금지하다
exclude from use, approach, mention, place under taboo

syn forbidden, prohibited 금지된 | prohibition, ban 금지 | forbid 금지시키다

The subject about other religions except Islam is still a taboo in their country.
이슬람교를 제외한 다른 종교는 여전히 그들 나라에서 금기시된다.

479 **alight**
[əláit]

v. [새 따위가] 내려 앉다, 착륙하다
come down and settle, as after flight

a. 불붙은, 빛나는
burning, lighted

syn land, perch, set down, get off 내려 앉다, 착륙하다, 내리다 | on fire, burning, lighted 불붙은, 빛나는, 등불이 켜진

He always alights(=gets off) at the same stop near his house. 그는 항상 그의 집에서 가까운 정거장에서 내린다.

The room was alight(=lighted) with lamps.
그 방은 등불이 켜져 있었다.

480 **detract**
[ditrǽkt]

v. 주의를 딴 데로 돌리다, [가치, 평판 등을] 떨어뜨리다
draw or take away; reduce the value, importance, or quality of something

syn diminish, reduce, lessen 줄이다

He was determined not to let anything detract his enjoyment of the trip.
그는 그 여행의 즐거움을 떨어뜨리는 것은 어떠한 것도 허락하지 않기로 작정했다.

detractor n. 중상자, 명예 훼손자

Word Root   ▶ tract = draw

attract	v. 매혹하다
contract	v. 수축시키다, 축소하다
distract	v. 주의를 흩뜨리다
extract	v. [노력, 힘으로] 뽑아내다, 짜내다
protract	v. 연장하다
retract	v. 철회하다
subtract	v. [수, 양을] 빼다, 공제하다
tractable	a. 다루기 쉬운, 유순한

Review

Monday

- ☐ intend _____
- ☐ pressing _____
- ☐ taboo _____
- ☐ loom _____
- ☐ mediate _____
- ☐ output _____
- ☐ recently _____
- ☐ provide _____
- ☐ seek (out) _____
- ☐ be in charge of _____
- ☐ manifestation _____
- ☐ relatively _____
- ☐ spot _____
- ☐ undertaking _____
- ☐ detract _____

- ☐ bare _____
- ☐ abhor _____
- ☐ string _____
- ☐ consort _____
- ☐ chamber _____
- ☐ distribute _____
- ☐ equivalent _____
- ☐ capricious _____
- ☐ extant _____
- ☐ alight _____
- ☐ fervor _____
- ☐ gather _____
- ☐ application _____
- ☐ defeat _____
- ☐ pioneering _____

481-510

481 **underway**
[ʌ̀ndərwéi]

a. 진행중인
in motion or operation; in progress

syn **continuing, going on, in progress** 계속되는

Rescue efforts are underway to find the lost climbers.
행방불명된 등산객을 찾기 위한 구조 노력은 계속되고 있다.

482 **patch**
[pætʃ]

n. 조각
a small piece of material affixed to another to mend or repair

v. 수선하다, 수습하다
put a patch on; repair something

syn **fragment, piece, scrap, square** 조각 | **mend, repair, fix** 수선하다, 고치다

She wore a sweater with patches on the elbows.
그녀는 팔꿈치를 수선한 스웨터를 입고 있다.

483 **absolutely**
[æ̀bsəlú:tli]

ad. 절대적으로, 무조건적으로
definitely and completely; unquestionably

syn **totally, entirely, definitely, completely, unconditionally** 완벽히

The food was absolutely fantastic. 그 음식은 정말 환상적이었다.

484 **ambition**
[æmbíʃən]

n. 야망, 목표
an eager strong desire to achieve something; the object or goal desired

syn **goal, aim, dream, hope, aspiration** 목표, 꿈, 열망

His ambition was always to become a successful writer.
그의 목표는 언제나 성공한 작가가 되는 것이었다.

485 **balance**
[bǽləns]

n. 균형, 조화, 안정
a state where things are of equal weight or force

syn **equilibrium** 평형 **stability** 안정

A new arms race in the region would upset the delicate balance between the opposing factions.

그 지역에서의 군비 경쟁은 적대 그룹 사이의 미묘한 평형을 뒤집어 놓을 것이다.

---

486 cast
[kæst]

v. 던지다
throw something

[syn] **throw, project, shed, radiate** 내던지다, 투사하다 **shape** 주조하다

The priceless treasures had been cast into the Mississippi.

그 값진 보물들이 미시시피 강에 내던져져 있었다.

---

487 complex
[kəmpléks]

a. 복잡한
consisting of interconnected parts

n. 종합
a whole composed of interconnected parts

[syn] **intricate, complicated** 복잡한 **elaborate, sophisticated** 정교한 | **group of buildings, sport complex** 종합운동장

This was a complex and difficult task.

이것은 복잡하고 난해한 과제였다.

---

488 design
[dizàin]

v. 디자인하다, 계획하다, 고안하다
create the design for; make a plan for; devise

[syn] **devise, fashion, plan, frame** 고안하다

A blood pressure is the force of blood flow that would move mercury in a specially designed narrow glass column.

혈압이란 특수하게 제작된 좁은 유리관에 들어 있는 수은을 이동시켰을 때의 혈류의 세기를 말한다.

designed a. 계획적인, 고의의　syn. intended, planned, intentional, deliberate, considered

---

489 effort
[éfərt]

n. 노력
the use of physical or mental energy to do something

[syn] **attempt, endeavor, exertion** 시도, 노력

The restructuring was part of an effort to boost company profits. 구조 조정은 회사의 이윤을 올리기 위한 노력의 일환이었다.

490 entire
[entàiər]

a. 완전한
having no part excluded

syn **whole, total, pure, complete, integral** 완전한

He gave his entire attention to the task in hand.
그는 손에 잡고 있는 일에 완전한 주의를 기울였다.

entirely ad. 전적으로 syn. completely

491 feature
[fíːtʃər]

n. 특성
a prominent aspect of something

syn **characteristic** 특질, 특성

The surface of Venus has many features similar to those on Earth. 금성의 표면은 지구의 것들과 비슷한 많은 특성을 갖고 있다.

492 flatten
[flǽtn]

v. 평평하게 하다
make flat or flatter

syn **level, even** 평평하게 하다, 고르게 하다, 평등하게 하다

This exercise helps to flatten a flabby stomach.
이 운동은 늘어진 위를 평평하게 하는 것을 도와준다.

flattened a. 평평한 syn. plain, plane, even
flat a. 평평한(having an even and horizontal surface; stretched out or lying at full length)

Plus Data
flattering a. 아부하는, 칭찬하는 syn. obsequious, praising

493 hold
[hould]

v. 갖고 있다
have and keep in one grasp

syn **contain, include, grasp, seize** 포함하다, 쥐고 있다

She is the first woman to hold this post.
그녀는 이 직위를 차지한 첫 번째 여성이다.

494 insolent
[ínsələnt]

a. 건방진, 무례한
insulting in manner or speech; disrespectful

syn **arrogant, rude, disrespectful, audacious, impertinent, impudent** 건방진, 무례한, 염치없는

After we had waited for long time, an insolent man tried to get in at the front of our position.

우리가 오랫동안 기다리고 있었을 때 한 염치없는 남자가 우리 앞자리로 끼여들었다.

Plus Data
polite(↔ insolent) a. 공손한

495 lay down

[syn] **put down, set down, build** 내려놓다, 비축하다, 세우다

The Natural Resources Department has laid down tough standards for water quality. 천연자원부는 깐깐한 수질 기준을 세웠다.

lay v. 놓다, 두다(place in or bring to a particular position)

Plus Data
lay off, dismiss, discharge, fire, depose 해고하다

496 matter
[mǽtər]

n. 물질, 문제
something that has mass and occupies space; problem

v. 중요하다
be important or affect what happens

[syn] **substance, material** 물질 **problem, issue** 문제점 | **be of importance, weigh** 중요하다

Teachers feel this is a matter for discussion with parents.
교사들은 이것은 부모과 상의해야 할 문제라고 생각한다.

497 nomadic
[noumǽdik]

a. 유목의
[of groups of people] tending to travel and change settlements frequently

[syn] **traveling, wandering, roaming, roving** 방랑하는 **itinerant** 순방[순회]하는

Arabian people lead a nomadic life.
아라비아 사람들은 유목생활을 한다.

498 pension
[pénʃən]

n. 연금
a sum of money paid regularly as a retirement benefit

[syn] **retirement fund, income** 연금, 수입

He started drawing his pension last year.

그는 작년에 연금을 받기 시작했다.

499 power
[páuər]

n. 능력

the ability or capacity to perform or act effectively

syn **strong effect, authority, strength, ability** 권세, 능력

Her parents still have a lot of power over her.
그녀의 부모는 아직도 그녀에게 막강한 영향력을 행사하고 있다.

500 perform
[pərfɔ́:rm]

v. 실행하다

do an action or piece of work

syn **carry out, execute, fulfill, accomplish** 실행하다, 완수하다

Machines are capable of performing many routine tasks.
기계로 많은 일상적인 일들을 처리할 수 있다.

Word Root	▶ form = norm
conform	v. 순응시키다 (to)
deform	v. 모양을 망치다
inform	v. ~에게 알리다
reform	v. 개혁하다
transform	v. 변형시키다

Similar Root	▶ firm = strong, hard
affirm	v. 확언[단언]하다
confirm	v. 확실히 하다, 승인하다
infirmity	n. 허약

501 scatter
[skǽtər]

v. 흩어지게 하다

[cause to] separate and go in different directions

syn **disperse, dissipate, spread, expel, dispel, radiate** 흩뜨리다, 퍼뜨리다

I scattered some grain on the floor of the hen house.
나는 닭장 바닥에 약간의 곡식을 뿌렸다.

502 reduce
[ridʒú:s]

v. 축소하다

bring down in extent, amount, or degree

syn **decrease, diminish, lessen, lower, shorten, abbreviate, shrink, contract, ease, moderate,**

recoil 줄이다, 낮추다, 단축하다, 완화시키다, 되돌아가게 하다

Many young Americans try to reduce the amount of fat in their diet. 많은 미국 젊은이들은 식사의 지방 함유량을 줄이려고 애쓴다.

reduction n. 축소

Word Root	▶ duce, duct = lead
conduce	v. ~에 공헌하다
deduce	v. 연역[추론]하다
induce	v. 꾀다, 설득하다
produce	v. 제조/생산하다
seduce	v. 유혹하다
abduct	v. (아이를) 유괴하다
deduct	v. (금액을) 빼다, 공제하다
education	v. 교육하다, 훈련하다
introduce	v. 소개하다

503 **seldom**
[séldəm]

ad. 드물게, 좀처럼 ~하지 않는
almost never, not often

syn **rarely, scarcely, hardly, barely** 거의 ~하지 않다

We seldom see each other anymore.
우리는 이제 거의 만나지 않는다.

504 **serve**
[sə:rv]

v. ~를 위해 일하다, [역할 · 기능을] 수행하다
work for; serve a purpose, role, or function

syn **assist, provide, work for** 돕다, 제공하다, 기여하다

Frank has served this company his whole working life.
프랭크는 직업 생활 전부를 이 회사에서 일했다.

505 **startling**
[stá:rtliŋ]

a. 놀라는, 깜짝 놀라게 하는
so remarkably different or sudden as to cause momentary shock or alarm

syn **unexpected, surprising, astonishing, amazing**
예상치 못한, 놀라운

Nobody made any response to his startling suggestion.
아무도 그의 뜻밖의 제안에 반응하지 않았다.

startle v. 놀라게 하다　syn. surprise, shock, alarm

506 summit
[sʌ́mit]

n. 정상
the highest point or part

syn **peak, highest point** 절정, 정상

They camped about 1,000 feet from the summit.
그들은 정상에서 1,000피트 떨어진 곳에서 야영했다.

507 tender
[téndər]

a. 부드러운, 섬세한, 다정한
fragile; young and vulnerable; caring and sympathetic

syn **soft, delicate, mild, gentle, temperate, modest, moderate** 섬세한, 온화한

He talks tough but has a tender heart.
그는 거칠게 말하지만 온화한 마음씨를 갖고 있다.

508 timid
[tímid]

a. 겁많은, 소심한
lacking self-confidence fearful and hesitant

syn **shy, nervous, timorous, fearful** 수줍어하는, 불안한, 소심한, 무서워하는

She gave me a timid smile. 그녀는 나에게 수줍은 미소를 지었다.

509 unadorned
[ʌ̀nədɔ́:rnd]

a. 꾸밈 없는
not decorated with something to increase its beauty or distinction

syn **plain, simple** 있는 그대로의, 간소한

He could not but make his rooms unadorned and dirty because of his busy work.
그는 일이 바쁘다 보니 방을 꾸미지도 못한 채 지저분하게 놔둘 수밖에 없었다.

adorn v. 장식하다 syn. decorate, ornate, embellish

> **Plus Data**
> decorated(↔ unadorned) a. 꾸민
> adore v. 찬양하다 syn. admire, respect

510 utterly
[ʌ́tərli]

ad. 완전히
to the full extent; completely

syn **completely, absolutely, totally, entirely, wholly**
완전히

Young children are utterly dependent on their parents.
어린아이들은 부모에게 전적으로 의존한다.

Review

Tuesday

☐ pension

☐ perform

☐ nomadic

☐ matter

☐ power

☐ seldom

☐ reduce

☐ scatter

☐ serve

☐ summit

☐ tender

☐ unadorned

☐ startling

☐ timid

☐ utterly

☐ patch

☐ absolutely

☐ underway

☐ ambition

☐ balance

☐ design

☐ complex

☐ effort

☐ entire

☐ feature

☐ cast

☐ hold

☐ flatten

☐ lay down

☐ insolent

511–540

511 vacant
[véikənt]

a. 비어 있는
containing nothing; not occupied

syn empty, unoccupied, blank, unfilled 텅 빈

The room on the first floor is vacant. 1층에 있는 그 방은 비어 있다.

512 vague
[veig]

a. 막연한, 애매한, 희미한
not clearly expressed; lacking definite shape, form, or character

syn imprecise, indefinite, unclear, obscure 분명하지 않은, 막연한 ambiguous, equivocal 애매한, 다의적인 indistinct 희미한

Witnesses gave only a vague description of the driver.
증인들은 운전자에 대해 막연한 진술만 했다.

> **Plus Data**
> definite(↔vague) a. 분명한 syn. noticeable, obvious, apparent

513 vital
[váitl]

a. 생명의, 생기있는, 절대로 필요한
of or relating to life; full of life; absolutely necessary

syn crucial, critical, necessary, principal, fundamental, essential 중요한, 근본적인

He played a vital role in setting up the organization.
그는 조직을 세우는 데 있어 중요한 역할을 하였다.

514 indispensable
[ìndispénsəbl]

a. 없어서는 안 되는
essential; absolutely necessary; unavoidable

syn essential, crucial, vital, necessary, required, important 필수적인

International cooperation is indispensable to resolving the problem of the drug trade.
국가간의 협력은 마약 거래 문제를 푸는 데 있어 필수적이다.

515 **ache**
  [eik]

v. 신체적인 고통을 느끼다, 동정하다
feel physical pain; feel sympathy or compassion

syn **hurt** 아프다 | **pain** 고통

All his limbs ached, and he shivered in the cold.
그는 수족이 모두 아팠고 추위에 몸이 떨렸다.

Plus Data

pains n. 수고, 노력 syn. care, effort, caution
take pains 수고하다, 애쓰다

516 **anonymous**
  [ənánəməs]

a. 익명의, 무명의
having no known name or identity or known source

syn **unknown, unidentified, nameless,
undistinguished** 알려지지 않은, 무명의, 유명하지 않은

The bomb threat was made by an anonymous caller.
그 폭탄 테러 협박은 익명의 전화에 의해 이루어졌다.

517 **assist**
  [əsíst]

v. 도와주다
give help or support to

syn **help, aid, support, conduce** 돕다

These measures were designed to assist people with
disabilities. 이 법안들은 장애우들을 돕기 위해 고안되었다.

518 **bore**
  [bɔ:r]

v. 구멍을 뚫다, 지루하게 하다
make a hole in; make weary by being dull, repetitive, or
tedious

syn **drill** 구멍을 뚫다

To eliminate insects that bore through furniture, they have
to use pesticide. 가구를 좀먹는 해충을 제거하려면 살충제를 써야 한다.

Plus Data

boring a. 지루한 syn. uninteresting, dull, tiring
bored a. 싫증나는, 피곤한 syn. uninterested, tired, weary
bear - bore - born 낳다, 생산하다

519 breathing
[bríːðiŋ]

n. 호흡

[syn] **respiration** 호흡

Julia was asleep, her breathing shallow but regular.
줄리아는 얕으나 규칙적인 숨을 쉬며 잠들어 있었다.

breathe v. 호흡하다 syn. inhale, respire

520 call for

v. 요구하다
require as useful, just, or proper

[syn] **require, demand, need, necessitate** 요구하다,
필요하다

By 1892 a Populist Party had appeared to call for free
coinage of silver to achieve this goal.
1892년에 이르러 민중당이 이 목적을 성취하고자 자유 은화제를 요구하며 등장했다.

521 commission
[kəmíʃən]

n. 위임, 임명, 직권, 임무
the act of granting authority to carry out a task or duty; the
authority so granted or the task so authorized

v. 위임하다, 위탁하다
grant a commission; place an order for

[syn] **charge, task, authority** 위임, 임무, 직권 | **appoint,
authorize** 임명하다, 위임하다 **engage, hire** 고용하다
permit 허가하다

He lost his commission due to ignoring to investigate the
event. 그는 그 사건을 조사하는 것을 무시한 일 때문에 직권을 박탈당했다.

522 conventional
[kənvénʃənl]

a. 관습적인, 통례적인
conforming to established practice or accepted standard;
based on general agreement, use, or practice

[syn] **usual, ordinary, routine** 일상적인 **traditional,
customary** 전통적인, 관습적인 **conservative** 보수적인
stereotyped 진부한

Her views are remarkably conventional.
그녀의 관점은 지나치게 보수적이다.

Plus Data
progressive(↔ conventional) a. 진보적인

523 detach
[ditǽtʃ]

v. 떼어내다, 분리하다
separate or unfasten; remove from association with

syn **separate, disconnect, remove, isolate** 떼어내다

A leaf detached itself from the tree and fell to the ground.
잎사귀 하나가 나무에서 땅으로 떨어졌다.

> **Plus Data**
> attach(↔ detach) v. 덧붙이다   syn. stick, bind, join, add

524 enlist
[enlíst]

v. 입대하다, 입대시키다
join the military; engage somebody to enter the army

syn **join in army** 군에 입대하다 **recruit, draft, enroll**
모집하다

In 1942, Louis enlisted as a soldier in Navy.
1942년 루이스는 해군에 입대했다.

525 extract
[ikstrǽkt]

v. 뽑아내다, 추론하다, 발췌하다
remove or take out something from

syn **remove, take out, extricate, elicit** 제거하다, 끄집어
내다, 구출하다, [진리·사실을] 도출하다

He opened a drawer and extracted a file.
그는 서랍을 열고 파일을 끄집어냈다.

526 forge
[fɔːrdʒ]

v. 위조하다, 꾸며내다, 만들다
make a copy of something with the intent to deceive; make or
produce

syn **make illegal copy, counterfeit, create** 위조하다,
만들다

The police are searching for stolen goods, forged passports,
and drugs. 경찰들은 장물과 위조 여권, 마약을 찾고 있다.

527 graze
[greiz]

v. 풀을 뜯다
feed on grasses

syn **feed, browse** 풀을 뜯어먹다, 방목하다

The sheep were grazing peacefully.
양들이 평화롭게 풀을 뜯고 있었다.

528 **wild**
[waild]

a. 야생의
occurring, growing, or living in a natural state

[syn] **uncultivated** [주로 식물의 경우] 야생의 **untamed,
undomesticated** [주로 동물의 경우] 길들지 않은

The wild rose is a familiar sight in woods and fields.
야생 장미는 숲이나 들판에서 흔히 볼 수 있다.

529 **juvenile**
[dʒúːvənl]

a. 소년[소녀]의, 유치한, 미숙한
of or relating to, characteristic of, or appropriate for children;
not fully grown or developed; young

[syn] **young, youthful, immature, childish** 어린, 젊은,
미숙한, 어린애 같은

When she was juvenile, her parents tried to make her a
great pianist.
어렸을 때 그녀의 부모는 그녀를 위대한 피아니스트로 만들기 위해 애썼었다.

530 **overall**
[óuvərɔ̀ːl]

a. 전부의, 포괄적인
from one end to the other; including everything; general
ad. 전반적으로, 종합적으로 봐서

[syn] **general, total, complete, comprehensive**
일반적인, 전체의, 종합적인 | **on the whole, as a whole, in
general, by and large, largely** 주로, 일반적으로

He was the senior police officer with overall responsibility
for the case.
그는 그 사건에 대해 전반적인 책임을 가지고 있는 고위 경찰 간부였다.

531 **mean**
[miːn]

v. 의미하다, 상징하다
be used to convey; act as a symbol of
a. 비열한, 심술궂은

[syn] **signify, imply, stand for, represent, indicate**
의미하다, 암시하다, 상징하다, 나타내다 | **humble, poor** 비천한, 초라한
of low grade 질이 낮은 | **unkind, cruel, malicious,
nasty** 몰인정한, 무자비한, 심술궂은, 비열한 | **stingy, miserly** 인색
한

What she means(=implies) is that there is no point in
waiting here. 그녀가 의미하는 것은 여기서 기다려봤자 소용없다는 것이다.

She has always been mean(=stingy) with money.

그녀는 돈에 대해 언제나 인색하다.

532 **paradox**
[pǽrədàks]

n. 모순
a self-contradiction

syn **contradiction, inconsistency** 모순, 불일치

We get this apparent paradox of people migrating to an area that has very high unemployment. 우리는 사람들이 실업률이 아주 높은 곳으로 이주하고 있는 외관상의 모순을 보게 된다.

533 **prosper**
[práspər]

v. 번창하다
to be fortunate or successful, esp. in terms of one finances

syn **flourish, thrive, progress** 번성하다, 발전하다

The business continues to prosper. 그 사업은 계속 번성하고 있다.

prosperity n. 번영 syn. wealth, opulence, riches

534 **prey**
[prei]

n. 먹이, 희생물
an animal hunted or caught for food; victim

syn **victim** 희생물, 먹이

Spiders usually catch their prey by building webs.
거미들은 보통 거미줄을 쳐서 그들의 먹이를 잡는다.

535 **put together**

v. 모으다, 구성하다
construct

syn **combine, compose, gather, congregate**
모으다, 구성하다

In building the fortification, we can put together a very strong case for the defense.
성곽을 지을 때, 우리는 방어를 위한 매우 강력한 경우들을 모을 수 있다.

536 range
[reindʒ]

v. 정렬하다, 배치하다, 변하다, 뻗치다
arrange in a particular order; change or be different within limits; extend in a particular direction

syn **vary, extend** 변동[변화]하다, ~의 범위에 미치다 | **scope, area, spectrum, variety** 범위, 영역, 변화

Costs range from 50 to several hundred dollars.
요금은 50달러에서 몇 백 달러까지이다.

537 scope
[skoup]

n. 범위, 활동 영역, 넓이, 지역
area covered by a given activity or subject

syn **range, extent, area, sphere, span, size** 범위, 분야, 활동 영역, 기간, 크기

There is still plenty of scope for improvement.
아직도 개선의 여지가 많다.

538 quit
[kwit]

v. 그만두다
depart or leave; stop doing a thing

syn **give up, abandon, relinquish, renounce** 포기하다 **stop, depart, leave** 그만두다 **resign** 사임하다

I was trying to quit smoking at the time.
나는 그때 담배를 끊으려고 했었다.

539 sensational
[senséiʃənl]

a. 선풍적인 인기의, 세상을 깜짝 놀라게 하는, 감각의
causing intense interest, curiosity, or emotion; of sensation

syn **exciting, amazing, startling, astounding, thrilling, marvelous** 흥미로운, 놀랄 만한

The team is still celebrating after their sensational Super Bowl victory.
그 팀은 파란을 일으킨 슈퍼볼 우승 이후 지금도 축제 분위기이다.

540 standard
[stǽndərd]

a. 표준의, 표준에 맞는
serving as or conforming to a standard of measurement or value

syn **unexceptional, normal, usual, regular, ordinary, customary, traditional, typical** 보통의, 통례의, 전형적인

It's a standard reply that the company sends out to applicants. 그것은 회사에서 지원자들에게 보내는 일률적인 답장이다.

Review

□ sensational _____

□ forge _____

□ graze _____

□ overall _____

□ wild _____

□ juvenile _____

□ paradox _____

□ prosper _____

□ mean _____

□ prey _____

□ put together _____

□ range _____

□ call for _____

□ standard _____

□ quit _____

□ vital _____

□ detach _____

□ vague _____

□ ache _____

□ extract _____

□ breathing _____

□ bore _____

□ anonymous _____

□ indispensable _____

□ commission _____

□ conventional _____

□ scope _____

□ enlist _____

□ vacant _____

□ assist _____

541-570

541 thus
[ðʌs]

[syn] hence, therefore, accordingly, consequently, as a result 따라서, 결과적으로

Someone had removed all the evidence. Thus, it was now impossible for the police to continue their investigation.
누군가가 모든 증거를 없앴다. 그래서 경찰이 조사를 계속하는 것은 이제 불가능하게 되었다.

542 underneath
[ʌndərníːθ]

prep. ~ 아래에
under or below

[syn] below, beneath, under 아래에

I'll leave the key underneath the mat.
나는 깔개 아래에 열쇠를 놔두겠다.

543 upheaval
[ʌphíːvəl]

n. 격변, 혼란, [땅의] 융기
a great change especially causing or involving much difficulty, activity, or trouble; a rise of land to a higher elevation a great change, disturbance, disorder, confusion,

[syn] disaster, catastrophe 대변혁, 혼란, 재난

There have been massive upheavals in the telecommunications industry.
통신 산업에 엄청난 변혁이 있어 왔다.

544 region
[ríːdʒən]

n. 지방, 지역, 영역
a particular area or part of the world, of the body, etc. or any of the large official area into which a country is divided

[syn] area, district, zone, territory, expanse, state
지역, 영역

Wages varied from region to region. 임금은 지역에 따라 달랐다.

545 **affectation**
[æfektéiʃən]

n. 겉치레, 과장
deliberate pretense or exaggerated display

syn **pretence** 겉치레, 가장

Lawson writes so well in plain English without fuss or affectation. 로손은 요란스럽지 않고 꾸밈 없이 쉬운 영어로 글을 매우 잘 쓴다.

> **Plus Data**
>
> **affection** n. 애착, 친교, 자애 syn. attachment, amity, fondness
> **affectionate** a. 애정이 있는 syn. loving, warm, friendly

546 **already**
[ɔ:lrédi]

ad. 지금까지
by this or a specified time

syn **earlier, formerly, previously, heretofore, by now** 이미, 지금까지

The gang leader had already left the country.
그 갱단 두목은 벌써 그 나라를 떠났다.

547 **ban**
[bæn]

v. 법으로 금지하다
prohibit esp. by official degree

syn **forbid, prohibit, bar, prevent, limit, control, check** 막다, 제한하다 **interfere, disrupt** 방해하다 | **veto, prohibition, prevention** 거부, 금지, 저지,

The book was banned at school libraries.
그 책은 학교 도서관에서 금지되었다.

548 **beverage**
[bévəridʒ]

n. 음료수
any liquids for drinking, usually excluding water

syn **drink** 음료

Government prohibited young students from buying alcoholic beverages.
정부는 어린 학생들의 알코올 음료 구매를 금지했다.

549 **choice**
[tʃɔis]

a. 특상의, 우량품의
of fine quality selected with care
n. 선택한 것, 대안
the one selected; an alternative

[syn] **optional, carefully selected** 선택의 | **selection, option** 선택한 것, 선택할 수 있는 것[옵션]

As a result Lincoln won the nomination by being the second choice of the majority.
결과적으로 링컨은 다수에게 제2의 선택이 됨으로써 지명을 받았다.

Plus Data
optional, selective 선택적인 ↔ required, compulsory, obligatory 의무적인

---

550 imitate
[ímətèit]

v. 모방하다, 흉내내다
copy the speech or behavior of someone or something

[syn] **copy, duplicate, replicate, mimic** 모방하다, 복사하다, 흉내내다

Italian ice cream is imitated all over the world.
이탈리아 아이스크림은 전세계에서 모방되고 있다.

imitated a. 가짜의, 모방의 syn. false, feigned, erroneous, incorrect, mistaken, wrong

Plus Data
identical a. 유사한, 닮은 syn. alike, indistinguishable, duplicate, the same

---

551 doctrine
[dáktrin]

n. 교리, 주의, 정책
a belief or system of beliefs accepted as authoritative by some group

[syn] **philosophy, principle, policy, act** 철학, 강령

The president announced the important doctrine for the best country.
그 대통령은 가장 살기 좋은 나라를 만들기 위한 중요한 강령을 발표했다.

---

552 curative
[kjúərətiv]

a. 병에 잘 듣는, 치료의
tending to cure; of or relating to the cure of disease

[syn] **healing, remedial, preventive** 치료의, 예방의

Ancient civilizations believed in the curative power of fresh air and sunlight.
고대 사회에서는 신선한 공기와 햇볕의 치유력을 믿었다.

Plus Data

incurable(↔ curative) a. 만성적인 syn. habitual, chronic

553 **dictate**
[díkteit]

v. 지시하다
prescribe with authority; speak as a superior

syn **determine, prescribe, require** 결정하다, 규정하다, 요구하다

Their choice was dictated by political circumstances.
그들의 선택은 정치적인 상황에 따라 결정되었다.

Word Root ▸ dic = say

edict	n. 명령, 칙령, 포고 [e⟨ex=out]
contradict	v. 반박하다, 모순되다 [contra=against]
dedicate	v. 바치다, 헌납하다
indicate	v. 가리키다, 나타내다
indict	v. 고발하다, 기소하다
predict	v. 예언하다

554 **endless**
[éndlis]

a. 끝이 없는
seemingly without end

syn **limitless, infinite, continuous, everlasting, eternal** 끝없는, 계속되는

They asked endless questions about our home town.
그들은 우리 고향에 대해 끊임없는 질문을 했다.

555 **examine**
[igzǽmin]

v. 주의 깊게 관찰하다, 분석하다
observe carefully; study or analyze

syn **inspect, look into, detect, investigate, scrutinize** 면밀히 살피다, 조사하다

She opened the suitcase and examined the contents.
그녀는 서류 가방을 열고 그 내용물을 조사했다.

556 **conflict**
[kánflikt]

n. 충돌, 갈등
a state of opposition between persons, ideas, or interests

syn **strife, struggle** 다툼 **clash** 충돌 **controversy** 논쟁 **discord, disagreement** 불일치

I try to avoid conflict whenever possible.
나는 가능한 충돌을 피하려고 노력한다.

conflicting a. 상충되는 syn. contradictory, opposing, contrary, inconsistent, incompatible

557 **finance**
[finǽns]

v. 자금을 공급하다
provide the money needed for something
n. 재정

[syn] **pay for, fund** 자금을 제공하다

The scheme is being financed by private enterprise.
그 계획은 민간 기업에게 자금을 제공 받았다.

558 **glue**
[glu:]

v. 붙이다
stick or fasten with or as if with glue

[syn] **stick, attach, paste, bond, fasten** 붙이다

You can glue stamps onto the card.
당신은 우표를 카드에 붙일 수 있다.

559 **colossal**
[kəlásəl]

a. 거대한, 엄청난
extremely large

[syn] **enormous, huge, immense, gigantic, titan, massive, vast** 거대한

It was a colossal waste of money. 그것은 엄청난 돈 낭비였다.

560 **incoherent**
[ìnkouhíərənt]

a. 일관성 없는
without logical or meaningful connection; unable to express one's thought clearly

[syn] **confused, jumbled, disorderly, disjointed, inconsistent** 혼란스런, 논리가 일관되지 않은

He could not make a precise decision at that time because of her incoherent mention.
그는 그녀의 일관성 없는 말 때문에 그 당시 정확한 결정을 내릴 수 없었다.

Plus Data

coherent(↔ incoherent) a. 논리적인, 일관된 syn. logical, reasoned, consistent

Word Root	▶ her = stick
adhere	v. [물건에] 부착하다
cohere	v. 밀착하다
inherent	a. 고유한, 선천적인, 타고난
inherit	v. 유산으로 물려주다
heritage	n. 유산
heredity	n. 유전

561 inspire
[inspàiər]

v. 고무하다, 영감을 주다

make someone feel that they want to do something and can do it

syn **motivate, encourage, stir, fire the imagination of** 동기를 주다, 격려하다, 북돋우다

Inspired by her example, other zoologists have begun working with apes in the wild.
그녀의 사례에 고무되어 다른 동물학자들은 야생 원숭이들을 연구하기 시작했다.

Word Root	spir = breathe
aspire	v. 열망·갈망하다
conspire	v. 공모하다
expire	v. [기간이] 다하다, 만료되다
perspire	v. 땀을 흘리다
respire	v. 호흡하다
spirit	n. 정신, 영혼
transpire	v. [비밀이] 밝혀지다 [몸, 식물이 수분을] 발산하다

562 lodge
[ladʒ]

v. 머물다, 숙박시키다

live in a place temporarily; provide housing for

syn **stay, accommodate, deposit** 머물다, 숙박시키다, 저장하다

The sword was still lodged in the old stone.
이 검은 여전히 오래된 돌에 박혀있다.

563 meager
[mí:gər]

a. 불충분한, 빈약한, 부적당한

deficient in amount, quality, or extent; barely adequate

syn **poor, scarce, scanty, insufficient, lacking** 빈약한, 결핍된

A meager food supply in the ship caused many hungry sailors to make severe troubles. 배에서 제공되는 빈약한 음식은 많

은 굶주린 선원들로 하여금 심각한 문제를 일으키게 만들었다.

564 minimize
[mínəmàiz]

v. 최소화하다
make small or insignificant

syn **decrease, curtail, diminish, reduce, lessen**
줄이다, 축소하다

You can try to minimize the damage to innocent civilians.
당신은 무고한 시민들이 받을 피해를 최소화하도록 노력할 수 있다.

565 outbreak
[áutbrèik]

n. 발발, 돌연한 출현, 폭발
a bursting forth, eruption

syn **beginning, occurrence, eruption** 시작, 발생, 폭발

An outbreak of food poisoning led to the deaths of five
people. 식중독의 발생이 다섯 명의 죽음으로 이어졌다.

566 nature
[néitʃər]

n. 성질, 자연

syn **characteristics, trait, inclination, disposition,
personality** 특성, 성향, 성격 **preference** 기호

They must understand the nature of a single cell animal
under the groundwater.
그들은 수중에 서식하는 단세포 동물의 특성을 이해해야 한다.

natural a. 타고난, 선천적인, 자연스런, 일반적인 syn. inborn, innate,
congenital, usual, ordinary, normal, likely(↔ acquired 후천적인)

567 permanent
[pə́:rmənənt]

a. 영구적인
lasting or remaining without essential change

syn **enduring, lasting, endless, unending,
perpetual, perennial, stable, fixed** 영구적인, 안정적인

He suffered permanent brain damage as a result of the
accident. 그는 사고로 영구적인 뇌 손상을 겪었다.

568 plume
[plu:m]

n. 깃털, 명예의 상징
a large feather

[syn] **feather, plumage** 깃털

Many birds have a variety of plumes according to their functions. 많은 새들은 기능에 따라 다양한 깃털을 가지고 있다.

569 **preclude**
[priklú:d]

v. 배제하다
to make impossible, esp. beforehand

[syn] **prevent, prohibit, forbid, hinder** 막다, 금하다

This policy precludes the routine use of pesticides.
이 정책은 살충제의 일반적인 사용을 막는다.

Word Root	▶ clude = shut
conclude	v. 결론을 내다
exclude	v. 빼다, 배제하다
include	v. 포함하다
seclude	v. 은거하다

570 **quaint**
[kweint]

a. 기묘한
charmingly odd, esp. in an old fashioned way

[syn] **odd, strange, unusual, extraordinary, unique**
이상한, 비범한, 독특한

As civilization develops more and more, quaint old customs were eliminated from leaders of their colony.
사회가 점점 더 발전할수록 식민지 지도자들에게서 이상하고 낡은 관습들이 사라진다.

Review

☐ glue

☐ incoherent

☐ quaint

☐ conflict

☐ finance

☐ inspire

☐ lodge

☐ colossal

☐ meager

☐ minimize

☐ nature

☐ plume

☐ curative

☐ preclude

☐ permanent

☐ beverage

☐ thus

☐ region

☐ underneath

☐ upheaval

☐ already

☐ ban

☐ imitate

☐ doctrine

☐ dictate

☐ outbreak

☐ examine

☐ endless

☐ affectation

☐ choice

571-600

571 **sufficient**
[səfíʃənt]

a. 충분한

being as much as is needed

[syn] **ample, enough, plentiful, adequate** 충분한, 적당한

He has the sufficient time to solve the hard problem.
그에게는 그 어려운 문제를 푸는 데 시간이 충분했다.

Word Root	▸ fac/fact, fec/fect, fic/fict = make
artifact	n. 인공물 [art=skill]
facilitate	v. 용이하게 하다, 수월하게 하다
factor	n. 요소, 요인
factual	a. 사실에 입각한
faculty	n. 능력, 교수진
manufacture	v. 제작[생산]하다
affect	v. ~에 영향을 미치다
defect	v. 이탈하다
effect	v. 초래하다
infect	v. ~에 감염시키다
perfect	v. 완전히 하다; 완전한
beneficial	a. 유리한
fiction	n. 허구, 소설, 이야기
proficient	a. 능숙한, 숙달된
suffice	v. 충분하다, 만족시키다 [suf⟨sub=under⟩]
superficial	a. 표면의, 외면의 [super=above, over]
sacrifice	v. 희생하다

572 **tenable**
[ténəbl]

a. 공격에 견딜 수 있는

capable of being maintained in argument; rationally defensible

[syn] **defendable, maintainable** 상태를 유지할 만한
secured, protected 안전이 보장된 **safe from assaults**
공격에도 끄떡 없는 **logical, practical, reasonable,**
justifiable, rational, viable 합당한

That kind of argument is no longer tenable.
이젠 그런 논쟁은 더 이상 말도 안 된다.

573 **undergo**
[ʌndərgóu]

v. 경험하다, 견디다

pass through [experience]; endure

196

syn **experience, suffer, endure, undertake** 겪다, 떠맡다

She underwent emergency surgery for suspected appendicitis. 그녀는 맹장염이 의심되어 긴급 수술을 받았다.

574 undisputed
[ʌ̀ndispjúːtid]

a. 의심할 바 없는, 명백한, 당연한
generally agreed upon

syn **unquestioned, undoubted, unchallenged, definite, clear, accepted** 의심할 것 없는, 분명한, 확실한, 받아들여지는

The facts of the case are undisputed.
이 사건의 사실들은 논쟁의 여지가 없다.

575 supplement
[sʌ́pləmənt]

n. 보충, 추가
something added to complete a thing

syn **addition, extension** 추가, 보충 | **add to, extend, complement, provide** 보충하다

By about 9,000 years ago, certain native-American peoples had begun to domesticate plants to supplement food that was foraged. 약 9,000년 전 채집해 온 식량을 보충하기 위해 인디언들은 식물을 재배하기 시작했다.

576 sparse
[spɑːrs]

a. 성긴, 부족한
not thick or dense

syn **scarce, scanty, bare, meager** 부족한, 빈약한

Higher up the mountain, houses became sparse.
산 위쪽에는 집들이 드물다.

Plus Data
abundant(↔ sparse) a. 많은 syn. rich, plentiful, ample

577 rotate
[róuteit]

v. 회전하다, 순환하다, 교대하다[시키다]
turn around on an axis or center; take turns or alternate

syn **alternate, turn, spin, whirl, swirl** 교대시키다, 빙빙 돌다

The Earth rotates 360 degrees every 24 hours.
지구는 24시간마다 360도 회전한다.

578 arbitrary
[ɑ́:rbitrèri]

a. 임의의, 독단적인
determined by chance and not by necessity

syn **random, chance, uninformed, capricious**
임의의, 우연의, 변덕스러운

The victims were not chosen arbitrarily.
희생자들은 무작위적으로 선택된 것이 아니었다.

579 aware
[əwɛ́ər]

a. 알고 있는
having realization or perception

syn **cognizant, conscious** 의식하는 **attentive, mindful**
주의 깊은

By nature, animals tend to be more aware of the dangers than human beings.
본능적으로 동물들은 인간보다 위험을 더 잘 알아차린다.

awareness n. 의식 syn. realization

580 burden
[bə́:rdn]

n. 짐, 책임, 의무
something that is carried; responsibility or duty

syn **responsibility, liability** 책임, 의무 **difficulty, problem** 어려움, 문제 **load, freight** 화물

Men say they are willing to share the burden of domestic work. 남자들은 집안 일이라는 부담을 기꺼이 덜겠다고 말한다.

burdensome a. 귀찮은, 성가신 syn. troublesome, annoying, irritating, disturbing

581 chiefly
[tʃí:fli]

ad. 주로, 대개
for the most part; above all

syn **mainly, dominantly, primarily** 주로, 대체로

There are branches of the store all over the country, but chiefly in the south.
그 상점은 지점이 전국에 있는데 남부에 주로 퍼져 있다.

582 complicated
[kámpləkèitid]

a. 복잡한
difficult to analyze or understand

syn **complex, involved, intricate** 복잡한, 뒤얽힌 **compound** 복합의

The situation seems to be getting more and more complicated. 상황이 점점 더 꼬이는 것 같다.

complicate v. 복잡하게 하다, 포함하다 syn. confound, entangle, involve

Plus Data
simple(↔ complicated) a. 단순한 syn. plain

---

583 **compose**
[kəmpóuz]

v. 구성하다, 작곡하다, 작문하다
form by putting together; produce music, poetry or formal writing

syn **create, make up, comprise, constitute** 구성하다 **draft, write** 쓰다

Muscle is composed of two different types of protein.
근육은 두 가지 서로 다른 단백질로 구성된다.

composition n. 구성, 작곡
composure n. 침착, 평정

Plus Data
composed a. 침착한 syn. calm

---

584 **demise**
[dimàiz]

n. 서거, 소멸, 폐지
death; the end of existence or activity

syn **death, decease** 사망 **end, expiration** 만기 **decline, fall, ruin** 쇠퇴

In this computer age, the better technology brings to the demise of many tools which were used a few years ago.
요즘 컴퓨터 시대에는 기술이 진보되어 불과 몇 년 전까지 사용되었던 많은 도구들이 더 이상 쓸모없게 되 버린다.

---

585 **hue**
[hju:]

n. 색, 색조
a color; a degree of lightness, darkness, strengths etc. of a color

syn **color, tint, shade** 빛깔, 색의 농담, 색조

They sought to find the natural hues in depicting their village. 그들은 고향을 그릴 때 자연스런 색조를 찾느라 애썼다.

586 **distant**
[dístənt]

a. [시간·장소가] 먼, 떨어진
separate in space or time; remote

[syn] **faraway, remote, aloof, removed, outlying**
거리가 먼, 떨어져 있는, 외진

Her eyes scanned the distant hills.
그녀는 멀리 언덕을 눈으로 훑었다.

587 **explicit**
[iksplísit]

a. 명백한
fully and clearly expressed

[syn] **clear, distinct, definite, precise, specific** 명백한,
분명한, 구체적인

From then on, the relationship between Stein's work and
painting became quite explicit.
그때부터 스타인의 일과 그림의 관계가 명확히 드러나게 되었다.

Plus Data
implicit(↔ explicit) a. 암묵적인, 불분명한 syn. ambiguous, equivocal,
vague, obscure, indefinite, unclear

588 **feeble**
[fí:bl]

a. 연약한, [빛·효과 등이] 약한
lacking strength; weak

[syn] **weak, fragile, frail, infirm, sickly, impotent,
ineffective, meager, poor, insignificant, insubstantial**
연약한, 허약한, 무력한, 빈약한, 하찮은

Don't be so feeble. Stand up to your nasty boss just for
once. 그렇게 약하게 굴지 마라. 고약한 사장에게 요번 한 번만 맞서 봐라.

Plus Data
strong(↔ feeble) a. 강인한 syn. healthy, robust, vigorous

589 **infrequent**
[infrí:kwənt]

a. 이따금 있는, 희귀한
not occurring regularly; occasional or rare

[syn] **intermittent, sporadic, unusual, periodical,
irregular** 간헐적인, 드문드문 일어나는

He was an infrequent visitor to the clinic.
그는 그 병원에 자주 가지 않았다.

590 **vile**
[vail]

a. 혐오스러운, 비열한
disgusting; unpleasant; morally depraved

syn **wicked, evil, mean, vulgar, bad** 악한, 비열한, 상스러운, 나쁜

The weather was really vile most of the time.
날씨가 내내 정말로 좋지 못하다.

591 **previous**
[príːviəs]

a. 앞의, 이전의
existing or occurring before something else

syn **earlier, prior, former, foregoing, preceding, past** 이전에

This issue was discussed in the previous chapter.
이 점은 이전 장에서 논의됐다.

592 **ingenious**
[indʒíːnjəs]

a. 독창적인, 영리한, 정교한
possessed of genius, or the faculty of invention

syn **creative** 독창적인 **bright, brilliant, clever, astute** 영리한 **adroit, deft, dexterous, expert, gifted** 솜씨 좋은

Animals were also caught by the Native Americans with a variety of ingenious nets and snares.
아메리카 원주민들은 갖가지 기발한 그물과 덫으로 짐승 사냥도 했다.

593 **involve**
[inválv]

v. 포함하다, 관여하다
contain as a part; engage as a participant

syn **include, contain** 포함하다 **entail** 수반하다 **pertain (to)** 속하다

Most research and development projects involve some element of risk.
대개의 연구와 개발 프로젝트들이 다소간의 위험 요소를 안고 있다.

594 marvel
[mάːrvəl]

n. 놀라운 일, 경이
something that causes surprise, admiration

v. 놀라다, 감탄하다
wonder, feel amazement or bewilderment at

syn **miracle, spectacle, wonder** 놀라움 | **be amazed, be astonished, be awed, wonder at** 놀라다

The magicians have done marvels for children.
마술사들이 어린아이들에게 놀라운 것들을 보여 주었다.

marvelous a. 놀라운, 굉장한 syn. wonderful, fantastic, spectacular, outstanding, remarkable, superb

595 overstate
[òuvərstéit]

v. 과장하다
enlarge beyond bounds or the truth

syn **exaggerate** 과장하다

He may have overstated his ability in the interview.
면접을 볼 때 그는 자신의 능력을 과장해서 말했던 것 같다.

596 penetrate
[pénətrèit]

v. 꿰뚫다, 관통하다
enter or force a way into

syn **enter, invade, pervade, infiltrate, permeate, saturate** 침입하다, 널리 퍼지다, 스며들다 **pierce, prick, puncture** 찌르다

A piece of glass had penetrated the skin.
유리 조각이 피부를 뚫고 들어갔다.

597 prescribe
[priskràib]

v. 규정하다, 지시하다
set down as a rule or guide; order the use of [a medicine or other treatment]

syn **dictate, assign, define, determine, establish**
지시하다, 정하다

The level of toxic chemicals was within the prescribed limits. 독극물의 수위가 허용치 안에 들었다.

prescribed a. 확정된 syn. certain, set, agreed, arranged, approved, given

598 **gigantic**
[dʒaigǽntik]

a. 거대한
very large or extensive

[syn] **huge, enormous, immense, colossal, gargantuan, monstrous** 거대한, 막대한

On the other hand, gigantic black holes may lie at the center of galaxies.
다른 한편, 거대한 블랙홀이 은하수 한가운데 있을지도 모른다.

599 **resort to**

v. 의지하다, 호소하다
turn to for assistance

[syn] **turn to, employ, exercise, utilize** 호소하다, 의존하다, 사용하다

I think we can solve this problem without resorting to legal action. 이 문제를 법률에 호소하지 않고도 해결할 수 있을 것 같다.

600 **display**
[displéi]

v. 보여주다, 전시하다
arrange something or a collection of things so that they can be seen by the public
n. 보여주기, 전시
a collection of objects arranged for people to look at;
a performance or show for people to watch

[syn] **show, unveil, demonstrate, exhibit** 나타내다, 증명[실연]하다, 전시하다 | **demonstration, presentation, show** 증명[실연], 발표, 전시

A unique display of ancient artifacts will be held in the national museum from next spring.
다음 봄부터 국립박물관에서 고대 유물 특별 전시회가 열릴 것이다.

Review

□ infrequent

□ explicit

□ distant

□ vile

□ marvel

□ chiefly

□ ingenious

□ arbitrary

□ display

□ burden

□ sufficient

□ gigantic

□ compose

□ resort to

□ penetrate

□ tenable

□ hue

□ feeble

□ undergo

□ undisrupted

□ rotate

□ sparse

□ involve

□ supplement

□ overstate

□ complicated

□ prescribe

□ demise

□ aware

□ previous

자연 II

의학, 컴퓨터 공학, 기술, 생물학, 동물학, 곤충학

Medicine

의학

ambidextrous 양손잡이의

amnesia 기억상실, 건망증

anatomy 해부학

anemia 빈혈

anesthesia 마취

antibiotic 항생물질의

antibody 항체

antidote 해독제

antiseptic 방부제

aorta 대동맥

artery 동맥

asthma 천식

barren 불임의 = sterile

belly 배, 복부 = abdomen

bowel 장

brain fag 신경쇠약

bronchi 기관지

carrier 보균자

cerebellum 소뇌

cerebral 뇌의

cerebrum 대뇌

chest 가슴 = thorax

chromosome 염색체

chronic 만성의 = habitual, incurable

circulatory system 순환기

coma 혼수상태

contagious 전염성의

dermatology 피부과

diabetes 당뇨병

diagnose 진단하다

disinfect 소독하다

dose 약의 1회분량

epidemic 전염병

epidermis 외피, 표피

excrement 배설물

gastric ulcer 위궤양

hereditary 유전의

hygiene 위생학

hypnosis 최면

indigestion 소화불량

insomnia 불면증

internal medicine 내과

intestine 창자

intoxication 중독

latency period 잠복기

leukemia 백혈병

limb 수족, 손발

malnutrition 영양실조

marrow 골수

membrane 막

nasal secretion (mucosa) 콧물

= nasal discharge

obesity 비만

obsession 강박관념

obstetrics 산부인과

orthopedics 정형외과

pain-killer 진통제

paralysis 마비

pediatrics 소아과

pharmaceutical 제약의, 약학의

plastic surgery 성형외과

pneumonia 폐렴

polio 소아마비

psychopath 정신병자

respiratory 호흡의

saliva 침

scurvy 괴혈병

sedative 진정제

segregation 격리, 분리

smallpox 천연두

sneeze 재채기

sore 상처, 종기

spinal cord 척수

stethoscope 청진기

stroke 뇌졸중

transfusion 수혈

trauma 외상, 쇼크

vaccination 예방접종

Computer Science
컴퓨터 공학

access time 접속에 걸리는 시간

assembler 어셈블러

capability 용량

compatible 호환성이 있는

computer specialist 컴퓨터 전문가

CPU(Central Processing Unit) 중앙처리
장치

decimal 십진법의

IC(Integrated Circuit) 집적회로

information retrieval 정보검색

memory bank 기억 장치

memory chip 메모리 칩

micro millennium 마이크로 시대

microchip 마이크로 칩

microcomputer center 컴퓨터 센터

microprocessor 마이크로 프로세서

office automation 사무자동화(OA)

optical memory 광 메모리

peripheral device 주변 장치

portable 들고 다닐 수 있는

store up 저장하다

terminal 단말기

Engineering
기술

abrasion 마모, 부식

application 용도

breakthrough 돌파, 타결

compression 압축, 응축

conductor 전도체

conduit 도관

corrosion 부식

elastic 탄성의

galvanic 전기의, 전류의

insulation 보온, 단열

laminate 막을 입히다

leakage 누전, 누출

mold 틀, 성형

obsolete 구식의, 쓸모없는

pilot 시험적인

polymer 고분자

prototype 표준, 모범

refraction 굴절

reinforcing 강화

resin 수지, 송진

soldering 땜질

tensile 장력

thermosetting 열경화성의

Biology

생물학

aerobic 유산소의

amino acid 아미노산

amphibians 양서류

anabolism 동화

anaerobic 무산소의

arthropods 절지동물

asexual reproduction 무성생식

atavism 격세유전

bark 나무 등의 껍질

biochemistry 생화학

birds 조류

chlorophyll 엽록소

chordates 척색동물

class 강

concentration 농축

conjugation 접합

crustacean 갑각류

DNA 디옥시리보핵산

egg 난자, 난세포

enmity 적의, 불화

enzyme 효소

evolution 진화

extinct 멸종한, 사멸한

extinction 멸종

family 과

fat 지방

fermentation 발효작용

fern 양치류

fertilization 수정

fishes 어류

game 사냥감

genetic 유전의

genus 속

gland 내분비 샘

glucose 포도당

heredity 유전

hermaphrodite 자웅동체

homeostasis 항상성

husk 과일 등의 껍질

insects 곤충류

intake 섭취

invertebrates 무척추동물

kingdom 계

larva 유충

limb 큰 가지

mammals 포유류

membrane 막

metabolism 신진대사

microbe 미생물

mineral 무기질

mutation 돌연변이

nervous system 신경계

nest 둥지

niche 서식지

nocturnal 야행성의

nucleic acid 핵산

offspring 자손

order 목

organism 유기체

pancreas 이자, 췌장

parasitic 기생석인

phylum 문

predator 포식동물

prey 먹이감

primate 영장류

protein 단백질

reproduction 생식, 번식

reptiles 파충류

respiration 호흡

rodent 설치류

secretion 분비

specious 종

sperm 정자

starch 전분

symbiotic 공생하는

taxonomy 분류학

tentacle 촉수

trait 특질

trunk 줄기

vertebrates 척추동물

yeast 효모

Zoology
동물학

adaptation 적응

aestivate 여름잠을 자다

arachnid 거미류

arthropod 절지동물

breed 번식하다

bug 벌레

capture 포획하다

carnivorous 육식의

centipede 지네

coelenterate 강장동물

cold-blooded 냉혈의

den 굴, 우리

dinosaur 공룡

dormant 동면의

flock 집단

habitat 서식지

herbivorous 초식의

herd 무리

hibernate 동면하다

leathery 가죽 같은

mate 짝을 짓다

woo, courtship 구애, 구혼, 짝짓기

migrate 이주하다

mollusk 연체동물

omnivore 잡식동물

predator 약탈자, 육식동물

prey 희생자

rodent 설치류

shell 껍데기, 외피

spine 등뼈, 척추

vertebrate 척추동물

saliva 침, 타액

wasp 장수말벌

Entomology

곤충학

ant 개미

antenna 더듬이

beetle 딱정벌레

butterfly 나비

caterpillar 애벌레

centipede 지네

cocoon 누에고치

colony (개미, 벌)한 떼

dragonfly 잠자리

firefly 반딧불

flea 벼룩

grasshopper 여치, 메뚜기

insect 곤충

insecticide 살충제

ladybug 무당벌레

locust 메뚜기

mandible 위턱

metamorphosis 변태

mosquito 모기

moth 나방

pollen 꽃가루, 화분

proboscis 주둥이, 입

pupa 번데기

Appendix

TOEFL에 꼭 나오는 동의어

동사

가장하다, 꾸미다, ~인 체하다	pretend, affect
강요하다	coerce, force, obtrude, extort, oblige, compel, demand, exact
거절하다	reject, decline, repudiate, refuse
고발하다, 고소하다	accuse, charge, impeach, arraign, incriminate, indict
과소평가하다	underestimate, understate, underrate, belittle
굽다, 휘다	bend, arch, crook
근절하다, 박멸하다	eliminate, eradicate, extirpate
기력이 빠지다, 쇠약해지다	debilitate, weaken, aggravate
꽃피우다, 번성하다	bloom, flourish, thrive, prosper
꾸짖다, 비난하다, 모욕하다	berate, scold, blame, insult, reproach, reprimand, censure, slander, affront
끌어내다	elicit, evoke, educe, extract
넓히다, 늘이다	expand, dilate, distend, extend, lengthen, stretch, draw out
달라붙다	stick, cling, adhere, cohere
당황하게 하다, 혼란시키다	confuse, perplex, embarrass, abash, jumble, dismay, bewilder
대체하다	supersede, replace, substitute, displace, take the place of
더럽히다, 오염시키다	pollute, contaminate, maculate, deface, besmirch
덧붙이다, 부과하다	add, appendix, annex, levy, impose
도망가다	flee, escape, abscond, run away, decamp
돌다	rotate, revolve, spin, swirl, whirl, hover
둘러싸다, 에워싸다	enclose, surround, encircle, besiege
등록하다	enroll, register, sign up, record, enlist, inscribe
만들어내다	coin, create, execute, produce
매혹하다, 부추기다	charm, attract, allure, entice, tempt, captivate, draw, lure, beguile, fascinate, bewitch
면제하다, 무죄로 하다	exonerate, exempt, free from blame, acquit, exculpate, remit ↔ incarcerate, imprison

모으다, 집합시키다	congregate, aggregate, convene, assemble, amass, rally, muster
못살게 굴다, 괴롭히다	harass, tease, bother, torment, torture, annoy, irritate
못하게 하다, 막다, 방해하다	dissuade, prevent, hinder, keep, discharge, disturb, hamper, block, bar, obstacle, prohibit, inhibit ↔ persuade, convince
문질러 없애버리다, 전멸시키다	rub out of, erase, annihilate, eliminate, get rid of, destroy, eradicate, nullify
반영하다, 숙고하다, 명상하다	meditate, muse, ponder, reflect, speculate, contemplate, think over, consider
배회하다, 방황하다	roam, wander, loiter, stray, rove, hover, ramble
변동하다, 진동하다, 망설이다	vacillate, fluctuate, oscillate, vibrate, waver, hesitate, shake, quake, scruple
비웃다, 조롱하다	deride, ridicule, mock, belittle, sneer, make fun of, tease disparage
빗나가다	swerve, deviate, deflect, digress, stray
빼다, 생략하다	omit, leave out, abridge
빼앗다, 제거하다, 면제하다	deprive, clear, remove, strip, rid, rob, acquit, dismantle
사기 치다	deceive
석화시키다	petrify, fossilize
세다	count, calculate, reckon
시작하다	originate, begin, initiate, launch, take off, embark, commence
싫어하다	detest, distaste, dislike, abhor, loathe, abominate, hate
싸우다	strife, conflict, struggle, emulate, contest, contend
아부하다, 아첨하다	flatter, compliment, blandish *cf.* bland 온순한
양보하다, 포기하다, 퇴위하다, 항복하다	renounce, yield, abolish, abandon, relinquish, cede, surrender, give up, waive, abdicate, desist, succumb, capitulate, forsake
여과하다, 거르다	percolate, pervade, penetrate, leach, filter, infiltrate, strain
연기하다	delay, postpone, prolong, procrastinate, put off, adjourn, defer
연루시키다	involve, entangle, entail, embroil
열망하다, 탐하다	crave, covet
울부짖다, 으르렁거리다	bark, howl, snarl
위안하다	console, condole, comfort, solace
유래하다, 기원하다	originate, flow out, issue from, stem from, derive from

응시하다	stare, gaze, watch
인용하다	quote, cite
일치하다, 동의하다, 조화하다	assent, accord, agree, accede, admit, consent, concord, concede, concur, conform, correspond (to) ↔ dissent, discord, disagree
자극하다, 충동하다	impulse, impel, arouse, actuate, stimulate, incite, spur
잡담하다	chat, gossip
적응하다, 조정하다	mediate, accommodate, adjust, adapt, acclimate, arbitrate, manipulate
전복시키다	overthrow, overturn, upside down, upset, capsize, upturn, subvert
조사하다, 검사하다	examine, inspect, scrutinize
존경하다	admire, adore, respect, worship, homage, esteem, venerate, revere
주장하다, 선언하다, 공포하다	claim, proclaim, declare, announce, herald, profess, assert, maintain, contend
줄이다	curtail, abate, lessen, decrease, contract, shrink from, recoil, ebb
지지하다, 떠받치다	support, bolster, prop, boost, foster
진정시키다, 달래다	appease, assuage, pacify, mollify, soothe, placate, allay, quell, lull
질식시키다	suffocate, choke, smother
찌푸리다, 찡그리다	frown, scowl
채굴하다, 발굴하다	mind, dig (up), excavate, unearth
추론하다, 암시하다	deduce, imply, infer, allude, hint, insinuate, connote
추방하다	exile, expel, oust, ostracize, banish *cf.* banish 사라지다 (=disappear)
충고하다, 훈계하다	advise, warn, caution, admonish
칭찬하다	praise, eulogize, extol, glorify, compliment, rave
타락시키다, 망가뜨리다	deteriorate, debase, degrade, degenerate, abase, stray, decline
투입하다, 침입하다, 위반하다	invade, breach, intrude, pierce, violate, encroach, infringe, breach, trespass
평가하다	assess, evaluate, estimate, rate, appreciate
할당하다, 분배하다	allocate, distribute, dispense

합병하다, 통합하다	unite, integrate, combine, merge, coalesce, amalgamate, confederate *cf.* M&A(=merge and acquisition) cartel, syndicate 기업연합
해고하다, 면직시키다	unseat, depose, dethrone, dismiss, discharge, fire out, lay off
협상하다, 타협하다	negotiate, compromise, bargain
호송하다, 호위하다	escort, convoy, guard
회피하다, 피하다	elude, dodge, avert, circumvent, escape, flee, evade
흥분하다, 자극하다, 기뻐하다	excite, elate, stimulate, exult
흩뜨리다, 분산하다	disperse, dissipate, spread, expel, dispel, diffuse, disseminate, scatter, radiate
힐끔 보다	glimpse, glance

명사

가정, 논문, 이론	treatise, thesis, theory
간단함, 짧음	abbreviation, brevity, shortness, laconism
개요, 개략	summary, synopsis, syllabus, epitome
결점	weakness, default, defect, fault, blemish
고통, 고뇌	agony, anguish, distress, pang
공감	compassion, sympathy, response
공적, 업적	feat, merit, accomplishment, achievement
구멍	hole, pit, pore, lacuna
구부러진	crooked, tortuous
구애, 구혼	courtship, mate, propose, court
낙담, 실망	disappointment, dejection, despondency
난국, 곤궁, 교착 상태	stalemate, deadlock, plight, predicament, dilemma
냉소, 조롱, 경멸	scoff, scorn, despise, contempt, contempt
당황, 황당	bewilderment, embarrassment *cf.* embrace 포옹하다
대소동, 혼란, 소요	tumult, turmoil, uproar, disturbance
도구, 기구	tool, apparatus, utensil, implement, instrument, appliance
도둑	robber, burglar, pilferer, thief
독백	soliloquy, monologue, aside

독재	tyranny, dictatorship, autocracy *cf.* autonomy 자치, 독립, 자율
명암, 밝기	visibility, intensity, brightness *cf.* brilliance 광택
무리, 떼	flock, herd, swam, crowd
반대자, 적	enemy, opponent, adversary, antagonist *cf.* protagonist 주인공
배신, 반란	treason, uprising, uproar
변덕	caprice, whim
부산물, 파생물	by-product, derivatives
분노	fury, anger, rage *cf.* be the rage 유행하다 furry 모피의
비방, 중상	blame, insult, scold, reproach, reprimand, defamation, disgrace, censure, slander *cf.* slender 낮은, 얇은
사기	deceit, cheat, trick, hoax
사본, 복사물	copy, duplicate, counterpart, transcript
서식지	habitat, dwelling place, station, haunt
선행, 앞섬	precedence, priority
속박, 구속, 노예	bondage, slavery, thrall
시작	dawn, onset, outset, beginning
신성, 거룩함	deity, divinity
암시	connotation, implication
열정	fervor, zeal, fever
영양분, 자양	nutrition, alimentation, nourishment, sustentation
용기, 인내심	courage, fortitude, bravery, boldness, patience, endurance
용모, 얼굴	guise, appearance, aspect
위험	danger, jeopardy, peril, hazard, risk
의복, 복장	clothing, costume, apparel, garment
인용, 발췌	excerpt, selected passage
절벽	cliff, precipice, bluff
정점, 천정	top, apex, peak, summit, vertex, pinnacle, apogee, zenith, acme, culmination ↔ nadir, lowest, point
존엄	dignity, majesty, prestige, grandeur, integrity *cf.* integrate 통합하다
좋은 감정, 호의	amity, friendship, good will ↔ enmity, hostility, antagonism, ill will, adversary

지명, 임명	appoint, nomination, designation ↔ dismiss, depose, fire, unseat
초보자, 견습공	beginner, novice, apprentice
충실, 충성	loyalty, fidelity, faithfulness, allegiance, homage
침입, 공격	incursion, aggression, invasion
탐욕	avidity, greediness, cupidity, avarice
특성, 특징, 성향, 습성	characteristic, trait, idiosyncrasy, trait, preference, inclination, tendency
틈	gap, chasm, cleft, crevice, hole, opening
포고령, 법령, 칙령	edict, ordinance, decree
허구, 꾸며낸 일	fiction, invention, figment
흠집, 얼룩	spot, splash, mar, blur

형용사

~하기 쉬운	apt, able, liable, facile, wieldy, be prone to, be disposed to, be apt to, be likely to, seem likely that
가려진, 숨겨진, 비밀의	hidden, secretive, cryptic, implicit, shrouded, confidential, underhanded
간결한	concise, terse, laconic, brief, pithy
강압적인	mandatory, compulsory, obligatory o optional, selective
거대한	huge, vast, massive, grand, gigantic, enormous, colossal, majestic
건조한, 마른, 척박한	arid, dry, barren, sterile, desiccated
검소한	economical, frugal, thrift, saving, sparing ↔ abundant, exuberant, extravagant, superfluous, profuse, prodigal, lavish
겁이 없는, 대담한, 용감한	brave, intrepid, daring, gallant, bold, fearless, dauntless, plucky
견줄 것이 없는	unequaled, unmatched, unrivaled, matchless, superior
고요한	serene, quiet, calm, still, tranquil, solemn, sedate, pacific, hushed, placid
근면한	diligent, industrious, assiduous *cf.* arduous 힘드는 ardent 열렬한
기본적인, 근본적인	cardinal, principle, chief, fundamental, prime, rudimentary,

	radical
끈질긴	persistent, tenacious, opinionated, stubborn, headstrong, obstinate, dogged
끊임없는, 지속적인	continual, continuous, constant, incessant, perpetual, permanent, unceasing ↔ temporary, passing, transient
나른한, 게으른	languid, sluggish, inactive, spiritless, stagnant, immobile, stationary
남자의	male, manly, virile
냉소적인, 비꼬는	cynical, sneering, caustic
넓게 펼쳐진, 포괄적인	extensive, comprehensive, panoramic
논리적인, 합리적인	logical, economical, reasonable, rational
놀랄 만한, 경탄할 만한	marvelous, stupendous, strikingly, wonderful, staggering
다산의, 풍부한	prolific, fertile, productive, fruitful, lucrative, ample ↔ barren, sterile
만성적인	chronic, habitual, incurable
맑은, 투명한	clear, transparent, limpid, lucid ↔ opaque, obscure, vague
목이 쉰	husky, horse, raucous
무딘, 무감각한	blunt, callous, indifferent, impervious
무시무시한	fearful, dreadful, dire, terrible, formidable, dismal, apprehensive
무자비한, 잔인한	ruthless, pitiless, merciless, cruel, hard-heart
민첩한, 활발한, 경쾌한	agile, active, brisk, frisky, lively, buoyant, cheerful, nimble
반란의, 배반의	insurgent, rebellious, treacherous
변덕스러운, 변하기 쉬운	shifting, changeable, fickle, capricious, whimsical, versatile, mutable
보조의	assistant, helpful, auxiliary, conducive
불법의	illicit, unlawful
빈약한, 부족한, 결핍된	meager, scanty
사심이 없는, 공정한	disinterested, impartial, fair, just
사악한, 나쁜	sinister, vicious, malicious, sinful, evil, heinous, diabolic(al), poignant, poisonous, harmful
살이 찐	obese, plump, fat cf. obesity 비만
상냥한, 친절한	friendly, amiable, affable, sociable, polite, genial
상서로운, 행운의	auspicious, favorable ↔ ominous, grim

생생한	graphic, vivid, picturesque, detailed
서두르는	hasty, rash, expeditious, hurried
서로의	reciprocal, mutual
서투른, 어색한	awkward, clumsy
솔직한	frank, outspoken, forthright, unfeigned, candid, sincere
시초의, 발단의	beginning, incipient, origin
신성한, 숭고한	holy, noble, sublime, dignified, sacred
신중한	discreet, careful, prudent, wary, deliberate, heedful
실현 가능한, 그럴듯한	feasible, plausible, possible, virtual, physical, practical, pragmatic, actual, specious
쓸모없는, 무익한, 사소한	futile, useless, trivial, trifling, unimportant, insignificant, negligible, petty, vain, minimal, slight
애매모호한	equivocal, ambiguous, indefinite, blurred, indistinct, vague, obscure ↔ apparent, obvious, definite, noticeable, tangible, perceptive
연속하는, 잇따르는	following, successive, ensuing, consecutive, subsequent cf. consequent 결국에
영리한, 간교한, 손재주가 있는, 숙달된	crafty, cute, wise, clever, sly, adroit, dexterous, cunning, canny, skillful, adept, proficient, shrewd, versatile
영적인	ghostly, spiritual
예비의, 잠정적인	provisional, preliminary, tentative
예의바른, 세련된, 멋진	chivalrous, courteous, urbane, sophisticated, refined, polished, stylish, chic
우호적인, 호의적인	favorable, genial, cordial, friendly
유명한, 현저한	famous, outstanding, renowned, conspicuous, prominent, noted, eminent, distinguished, exalted, celebrated
융통성 있는, 탄력적인	pliable, elastic, flexible, resilient
의도적인, 고의의	intentional, deliberate, purposed ↔ casual
의심 많은	incredulous, skeptical, doubtful
이상한	odd, extraordinary, grotesque, eccentric, quaint, peculiar, uncommon, queer, unusual, strange, unique, bizarre
익살맞은, 우스운	funny, witty, facetious, humorous
인색한	stingy, miserly
인식하는, 알고 있는	aware, conscious, cognizant
잘못된, 그릇된, 거짓의	false, fallacious, pseudo, pretended, spurious

저속한, 음탕한	vulgar, obscene
전형적인, 판에 박힌, 상투적인	stereotyped, conventional, routine, lacking, originality, typical, trite
정기적인, 간헐적인	irregular, infrequent, sporadic, intermittent, periodic
즉흥적인	impromptu, ad lib, offhand *cf.* impromptus 즉석 연주 improvise 즉석에서 만들다
치명적인	deadly, fatal, lethal, mortal
타고난, 선천적인	innate, inborn, natural, intrinsic, congenital *cf.* congenial 마음이 같은
틀림없는, 확실한	unerring, unfailing, steadfast, steady
퍼지는, 유행하는	prevailing, prevalent, dominant, overwhelming, infectious, epidemic, contagious
평행의, 나란히, 병치의	abreast, parallel *cf.* juxtapose 나란히 놓다
표면상, 겉보기에	seeming, apparent, superficial, ostensible *cf.* ostentatious 잘난 척하는
피할 수 없는, 필수적인	inevitable, essential, unavoidable
해롭지 않은	innoxiously, harmless, innocuous
호전적인	warlike, bellicose, belligerent, quarrelsome, pugnacious
홍수, 재난, 재앙	inundation, flood, cataclysm, deluge *cf.* divulge 폭로하다

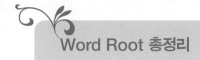

Word Root 총정리

ann = year
p.130

annual a. 일년의

annually ad. 일년마다

semiannual a. 반년마다의

anniversary n. 해마다 돌아오는 기념일

biennial a. 2년마다의 bi - 2

decennial a. 10년마다의 dece - 10

centennial a. 100년마다의 cente - 100

bicentennial a. 200년마다의 bicente - 200

perennial a. 계속되는 per - 계속

ced, cess = go
p.21

access n. 접근, 출입, 통로

accede v. (요구, 제안 등에) 동의하다

cease v. 그만두다, 중단하다

cede v. (권리, 영토 등을 다른 나라에) 양도하다

concede v. 인정·용인하다

exceed v. 능가하다

precede v. (시간, 장소, 순서에서) 앞서다

proceed v. 앞으로 나아가다

process v. (식품을) 가공처리 하다

recede v. 물러나다, 퇴각하다

secede v. 탈퇴(이탈)하다 (se = away, apart)

succeed v. 성공하다, 계승하다

cept, ceiv, ceit = take
p.31

conceive v. (생각, 계획 등을) 마음에 품다, 구상하다

deceive v. 속이다

perceive v. 지각(인식)하다

receive v. 받다

cis = cut
p.100, 112

concise a. 간결한 (con = intensive, together)

decisive a. 결정적인, 단호한 (de = down)

excise v. (몸의 일부를) 잘라내다, (문장 따위를) 삭제하다

incise v. 절개하다, 조각하다 (in = in, into)

precise a. 정밀한, 꼼꼼한 (pre = before, intensive)

clude = shut
p.148, 194

exclude v. 배제하다, 빼다 (ex = out)

conclude v. 결론짓다 (con = together)

include v. 포함하다

seclude v. 격리시키다, 은퇴하다 (se = away, apart)

preclude v. 막다, 방해하다 (pre = before)

cord = heart
p.10

accord v. 일치하다, 조화하다

concord n. 일치, 화합

discord n. 불일치, 불화

sent = feel
p.10

assent v. (제안에) 찬성하다

consent v. 동의(찬성)하다

dissent v. 반대하다

resent v. 분개하다

sentimental a. 감정적인

cur = run
p.130

concur v. 동시에 일어나다

incur v. 자초하다, 초래하다

occur v. 일어나다, 발생하다

current a. 현재의 n. 흐름, 경향, 추세

recur v. 재발하다, 회상하다

dic = say p.190

edict n. 명령, 칙령, 포고(e〈ex = out〉)

dictate v. 받아쓰게 하다, 지시하다

contradict v. 반박하다, 모순되다(contra = against)

dedicate v. 바치다, 헌납하다

indicate v. 가리키다, 나타내다

indict v. 고발하다, 기소하다

predict v. 예언하다

duce, duct = lead p.174

conduce v. ~에 공헌하다

deduce v. 연역(추론)하다

induce v. 꾀다, 설득하다

produce v. 제조(생산)하다

reduce v. 축소하다

seduce v. 유혹하다

abduct v. (아이를) 유괴하다

deduct v. (금액을) 빼다, 공제하다

education v. 교육하다, 훈련하다

introduce v. 소개하다

fac/fact, fec/fect, fic/fict = make p.28, 196

artifact n. 인공물(art = skill)

facilitate v. 용이하게 하다, 수월하게 하다

factor n. 요소, 요인

factual a. 사실에 입각한

faculty n. 능력, 교수진

manufacture v. 제작(생산)하다

affect v. ~에 영향을 미치다

defect v. 이탈하다

effect v. 초래하다

infect v. ~에 감염시키다

perfect v. 완전히 하다 a. 완전한

beneficial a. 유리한

fiction n. 허구, 소설, 이야기

proficient a. 능숙한, 숙달된

suffice v. 충분하다, 만족시키다(suf〈sub = under〉)

superficial a. 표면의, 외면의(super = above, over)

sacrifice v. 희생하다

fer = carry p.125

confer v. 주다, 모으다

defer v. 연기하다, 늦추다

differ v. 의견이 다르다

indifferent a. 무관심한, 냉담한

infer v. 추리, 추론하다

interfere v. 간섭, 참견하다

offer v. 제공하다

prefer v. 오히려 ~을 택하다, 좋아하다(pre = before)

refer v. 언급(암시)하다

suffer v. (고통 따위를) 입다, 겪다

transfer n. 이전 v. 옮기다

fertile a. (토지 따위가) 비옥한

form = norm p. 42, 173

conform v. 순응시키다 (to)

deform v. 모양을 망치다

inform v. ~에게 알리다

reform v. 개혁하다

transform v. 변형시키다

fus = pour p. 72

effusion n. (사상, 감정 등의) 용솟음, 토로

confuse v. 혼란시키다

diffuse v. (빛 따위를) 발산하다

infuse v. (액체를) 주입하다

fuse v. 융합시키다

refuse v. 거절하다

profuse a. 많은, 아낌없는

gen = birth, creation, race, kind
p.37, 84

congenial a. 같은 성질의, 마음 맞는

congenital a. (병 따위가) 선천적인

engender v. 발생시키다, 야기하다

homogeneous a. 동종의(homo, iso = same)

ingenious a. (사람이) 영리한

genial a. (날씨 등이) 성장에 맞는, 온화한, 따뜻한, 친절한, 다정한

generate v. 낳다, 산출하다, 야기하다

degenerate v. 타락(퇴보)하다

genius n. 천재, (타고난) 자질, 경향, 특징

general a. 일반적인

genuine a. 진짜의

genetic a. 유전학의

gest = carry
p.131

ingest v. (음식물 등을) 섭취하다

congestion n. 혼잡

digest v. 소화하다

register n. 기록부, 등록

suggest v. 제안하다, 암시하다

hab, hib = live
p.48

habitual a. 습관의, 버릇이 된

habitat n. (동식물의) 산지, 서식지

inhabitant n. 거주자, 서식 동물

exhibit v. 보여주다

inhibit v. 방해하다, 억제하다(in = not)

prohibit n. 금지하다

her = stick
p.148, 192

cohere v. 밀착하다, 앞뒤 논리가 맞다

inhere v. 타고나다

inherent a. 고유한, 선천적인

inherit v. 유산으로 물려주다

heritage n. 유산

heredity n. 유전

ject = throw
p.123

conjecture v. 추측하다

deject v. 슬프게 하다, 실망하다

ejaculate v. 사출하다

inject v. (액체, 약 따위를) 주사하다

interject v. (말 따위를) 불쑥 끼워 넣다

object n. 목적 v. 반대하다

project v. 계획하다, 발사하다

reject v. 거절하다

subject n. 주제, 학과

nounce, nounci = say
p. 25

announce v. 발표하다, 알리다

denounce v. 공공연히 비난하다, 고발하다

pronounce v. 발표하다

renounce v. (권리 등을) 포기하다, 부인하다

enunciate v. 말하다, 발음하다

pel, peal, puls = drive
p.49, 116

compel v. 억지로 ~을 시키다

compulsory a. 의무적인

dispel v. (불길한 생각을) 쫓아버리다, 분산시키다

expel v. 내쫓다

impel v. 추진시키다

impulse n. 추진(력)

propel v. 추진하다

repel v. 쫓아버리다, 불쾌감을 일으키다

repulse v. 쫓아버리다

repellent a. 불쾌한

pli, ply, ple, plet = fill   p.33

accomplish v. 이루다

compliment n. v. 칭찬(하다)

complement n. v. 보완(하다)

complete a. 완전한 v. 완성하다

deplete v. 고갈시키다

implement n. 도구 v. 약속을 이행하다

supplement n. v. 보충(하다)

plic, ply = fold   p.42

apply v. 신청하다

applicable a. 적용할 수 있는, 적절한

complicate v. 복잡하게 하다

explicate v. (상세히) 설명하다(ex = out)

employ v. 고용하다

imply v. 함축하다

implicate v. (사건, 범죄에) 관련되다

implicit a. 은밀한, 함축적인

simplicity n. 단순, 간단

pos = put   p.74

compose v. 구성하다, 쓰다

oppose v. ~에 반대하다

depose v. (국왕을) 폐하다, 면직하다

purpose n. 목적, 의도

expose v. 노출시키다

suppose v. 가정하다, 추측하다

impose v. (세금 따위를) 부과하다

prehens, prehend = take   p.32

apprehend v. 체포하다, 염려하다

comprehend v. 이해하다

comprehensive a. 포괄적인, 포용력이 큰

rup = break   p.29, 77

bankrupt a. 파산한, 지급능력이 없는(bank = bench)

corrupt v. 부패시키다(cor〈con = together)

erupt v. (화산 등이) 폭발하다

disrupt v. 분열시키다, 막다

interrupt v. 중단시키다, 가로막다(inter = between)

rupture n. 파열, 불화

scend, scan, scent = climb   p.128

ascend v. 오르다(a = up)

condescend v. 검손하게 자세를 낮추다(con = together), (de = down)

descent n. 가계, 혈통, 하강

transcend v. 초월하다(trans = to pass)

transcendent a. 뛰어난

transcendental a. 초자연적인

transcendentalism n. 초월주의, 선험주의

scrib / script = write   p.203

ascribe v. (원인 따위를) ~으로 돌리다

circumscribe v. 한계를 정하다(circum = around)

describe v. 묘사하다(= depict)

inscribe v. 쓰다, 새기다

prescribe v. 규정하다, 지시하다

proscribe v. 금지하다, 인권을 박탈하다

subscribe v. (돈을) 기부하다, 동의하다(sub=under)

transcribe v. 베끼다, 복사하다

sist = stand p.68

assist v. 돕다, 공헌하다

consist v. ~으로 이루어지다

desist v. 그만두다, 중지하다

insist v. 주장하다

persist v. 지속하다, 고집하다

resist v. 저항하다, 반대하다

subsist v. 생존하다, 살아가다

spect = see p.152

aspect n. 양상, 국면

circumspect a. 신중한, 주의 깊은(circum=around)

expect v. 기대하다, 예상하다

inspect v. 검사(조사)하다

introspect v. 내성(자기 관찰)하다(intro=within)

respect n. 존경, 경의(re=again)

retrospect n. 회고, 회상(retro=backward)

suspect v. 의심하다(sus/sub=under)

spir = breathe p.192

aspire v. 열망ㆍ갈망하다

conspire v. 공모하다

expire v. (기간이) 다하다, 만료되다

perspective n. 관점, 조망

perspire v. 땀을 흘리다

respire v. 호흡하다

spirit n. 정신, 영혼

transpire v. (비밀이) 밝혀지다, (몸, 식물이 수분을)
발산하다

tain = get p.19

abstain v. 삼가하다, 억제하다(abs=off, away)

attain v. 이루다

contain v. 포함하다(con=together)

detain v. 붙들다, 구류하다(de=down)

entertain v. 즐겁게 하다

maintain v. 유지하다

obtain v. 얻다, 획득하다

pertain v. 속하다, 관계하다

retain v. 보유하다

sustain v. 떠받치다, 부양하다(sus(=sub)=under)

termin = end, limit, boundary
p.143

exterminate v. 근절하다(ex=out)

determine v. 결정(결심)하다(de=away)

interminable a. 지루한, 끊임없는(in=not)

terminate v. 종결을 짓다, 끝내다

terminal n. 터미널

terminology n. 전문 용어

tract = draw p.93, 167

attract v. 매혹하다

contract v. 수축시키다, 축소하다 n. 계약

detract v. 명성을 떨어뜨리다

extract v. (노력, 힘으로) 뽑아내다

protract v. 연장하다

retract v. 철회하다

subtract v. (수, 양을) 빼다(sub=under)

tractable a. 다루기 쉬운, 유순한

tribut = give p.162, 173

attribute n. 속성, 특질

attribute v. ~에 기인하다

contribute v. 기여(기부)하다

tributary a. 공물을 바치는, 지류의

firm = strong, hard   p.173

affirm v. 확언(단언)하다

confirm v. 확실히 하다, 승인하다

infirmity n. 허약

tric, trigu = petty obstacle   p.102

extricate v. (위험 · 곤경으로부터) 구출하다, 해방하다

intricate a. 뒤얽힌, 복잡한

intrigue v. 흥미를 유발시키다

trud, trus = thrust   p.85

abstruse a. 난해한(abs(ab = away)

extrude v. (사람, 물건을) 밀어내다

intrude v. 강요하다, 침입하다

protrude v. 내밀다

und, ound = wave   p.81

abound v. 풍부하다, 가득 채우다

inundate v. 범람시키다

redundant a. 남아도는

surround v. 에워싸다, 둘러싸다

undulate v. (파도처럼) 움직이다

vent, ven = come   p.90

advent n. 출현, 도래

circumvent v. (계획을) 방해하다, (법, 규칙, 어려움 따위를) 회피하다(circum = around)

convene v. (모임 따위를) 소집하다

invent v. 발명하다, 고안하다

intervene v. 간섭하다, 조정(중재)하다

prevent v. 막다(방해)하다

vert, vers = turn   p.35

adverse a. 반대하는, 불리한

avert v. (눈, 얼굴, 생각 등을) 돌리다, (위험을) 피하다

adversary n. 적, 상대자

converse a. 거꾸로 n. 반대

convert v. 개종(전환)하다

controvert v. 반박(논쟁)하다

controversy n. 논쟁, 논의

incontrovertible a. 논쟁의 여지가 없는

invert v. 뒤집다

revert v. (원상태로) 되돌아가다

subvert v. (종교, 정부를) 파괴하다, 전복시키다 (sub = below)

vertical a. 수직의, 바로선

vict, vinc = conquer   p.82

convict v. 유죄로 선고하다(con = intensive) n. 기결수

convince v. 확신하게 하다

evict v. (토지에서 세든 사람을) 쫓아내다(e = out)

evince v. (감정 따위를) 나타내다

invincible a. 정복할 수 없는(in = not)

suspend v. 중단시키다, 매달다

vanquish v. 정복하다(vanq(vanc(vinc)

victim n. 희생자

victory n. 승리자, 정복자

voc, vok = call   p.38

advocate v. 지지하다, 옹호하다

convoke v. (회의를) 소집하다

equivocal a. 이중 의미의, 애매한(equ = same)

evoke v. (법에) 호소하다, 영혼을 불러내다

irrevocable a. 최종적인, 철회할 수 없는

provoke v. 성나게 하다, 도발하다

revoke v. (명령, 동의, 허가를) 철회(취소)하다
　　　　　[re＝back]

suggest v. 암시하다, 제의하다

vocation n. 직업(옛날에는 하늘이 부른 것을 천직
　　　　　이라 했음)

INDEX 표제어

B

C

D

engage syn. hire, involve, apply

enhance syn. improve, exalt, increase, augment

enlist syn. join in army, recruit, draft, enroll

enormous syn. huge, immense, tremendous, vast, great

entail syn. involve, require

enter syn. go into, come in

enthusiasm syn. intense interest, passion, fervor, zeal

entire syn. whole, total, pure, complete, integral

environment syn. ecology, setting, surroundings, habitat

equivalent syn. comparable, corresponding, equal, interchangeable

eradicate syn. eliminate, wipe out, get rid of

erect syn. raise, build, construct

erratic syn. irregular, inconsistent, shifting

especially syn. specifically, particularly, notably

establish syn. settle, confirm, constitute, organize, start

estimate syn. calculate roughly, judge, predict, evaluate, appreciate

even syn. unchanging, plain, impartial

eventually syn. finally, later

evidence syn. proof, reveal | prove, manifest

evident syn. apparent, noticeable, obvious, perceptible, definite

examine syn. inspect, look into, detect, investigate, scrutinize

exceed syn. surpass, go beyond

exception syn. exclusion

excluding syn. without, not including, other than, except, but

exercise syn. practice, use | workout

exhibit syn. feature, present, show, display

expand syn. increase, enlarge, inflate, spread out

expertise syn. special skill, ability

explicit syn. clear, definite, distinct, precise, specific

exploit syn. use, employ, utilize, manipulate

I

J

K

meticulous syn. careful, painstaking, detailed p.151

migrate syn. travel, shift, move long distance from one place to another p.49

mimic syn. imitate, copy, mirror p.49

minimize syn. decrease, curtail, diminish, reduce, lessen p.193

miniscule syn. tiny, minor, minute p.13

mode syn. form, method, fashion, scale p.63

modification syn. alteration, change p.19

monitor syn. check, govern, control, supervise p.115

moreover syn. additionally, in addition, furthermore p.102

motif syn. theme, concept, topic, design, pattern, figure p.89

mounting syn. increasing, rising, growing, escalating p.133

myriad syn. many, numerous, innumerable n. variety p.130

N

nature syn. characteristics, trait, inclination, disposition, personality, preference p.193

negligible syn. insignificant, unimportant, trivial, trifle, minimal p.142

network syn. set of connection, system p.86

nomadic syn. traveling, wandering, roaming, roving, itinerant p.172

notion syn. concept, idea, opinion p.75

novel syn. unusual, new, strange p.65

noxious syn. harmful, poisonous, poignant, vicious p.75

O

object syn. purpose, goal, aim, thing, material p.122

obscure syn. ambiguous, equivocal, vague, uncertain, dim | conceal, darken, dim, overshadow, eclipse, camouflage, cloak, shroud p.14

obsolete syn. old fashioned, out of fashion, unused, antiquated p.82

obtain syn. achieve, attain, gain, acquire, capture, grasp p.40

obvious syn. apparent, evident, manifest p.24

P

Q

R

S

T

U

V

W

Y